THERE GOES T.

1st Edition

Published in 2012 by
Woodfield Publishing Ltd
Bognor Regis PO21 5EL England
www.woodfieldpublishing.co.uk

ISBN 1-84683-144-X

Printed and bound in England
Typesetting & page design by Nicolai Pastorius
Cover design by Klaus Berger

There Goes the Siren

*Childhood memories of the London
Blitz and Wartime Evacuation*

S<small>HEILA</small> L<small>EMMER</small> D<small>OBSON</small>

Woodfield

Woodfield Publishing Ltd

Bognor Regis ~ West Sussex ~ England ~ PO21 5EL
tel 01243 821234 ~ **e/m** info@woodfieldpublishing.co.uk

Interesting and informative books on a variety of subjects

For full details of all our published titles, visit our website at
www.woodfieldpublishing.co.uk

*I dedicate this book to my dear Mother,
in respect of the loving care and stalwart courage she
showed, which helped to carry us through the dark
days of the war, to all the ladies who helped to keep the
home fires burning and to the husbands, fathers,
brothers and sons for the sacrifices they made to save
our country from tyranny.*

~ CONTENTS ~

Acknowledgements

I would like to thank the charming young lady doctor at Shrewsbury Hospital and retired teacher Mrs. Jo Harris, without whose suggestion and encouragement I would not have considered publishing this book; Cheryl and Edmund Gerdes Hansen and Frank Rixon for their assistance in its publication and, lastly, my dear husband Peter, whose patience, advice and encouragement assisted me through the difficulties of writing, production and publication.

Preface

The following incidents and experiences of evacuation and the war are as seen through the eyes and mind of a child between the ages of four to ten years. I have tried to be as honest as possible and stick strictly to what I remember. However, there are one or two incidents which have been related to me by an older family member, which I am fairly certain are also true. If anyone disagrees, I apologise. With regard to chapter ten, I am including my own more mature experiences and understanding as I am concerned with the condition of the planet and recognize that the war we now face is the prevention of its destruction.

I owe much to a very young curate (at the time), Reverend Chris Gonin, through whom I eventually discovered Jung's Analytical Psychology, via The Open Way Charitable Trust- and a wonderful analyst, Mrs Carol Jeffrey, with whom I was asked to "work" as what she called a "student" because she felt that I had a very enquiring mind. I did not become an analyst, as she wished, but I did study for an honours degree and became a teacher, although I eventually trained as a bereavement counsellor. Much of what I learned was not by direct teaching but by gentle listening, suggestion and guidance by Carol, to whom I am extremely grateful as she recognized my search for Truth. I became and remained a member of the Open Way Charitable Trust for many years until it became amalgamated with The Guild of Pastoral Psychology, of which I am still a member.

1.   The Warning

"There goes the siren," she thought, "right on time." She was hoping the Air Raid Warning would be a bit late tonight because it would upset the girls, whereas, if they were already asleep it didn't seem to wake them. Oh well, it couldn't be helped...

She quickly finished making the jug of cocoa and took it, with the bag of biscuits, into the Anderson shelter in the garden, where her three daughters were already settling down for the night. Emmie was the eldest. She was seven years old. Marie was five years and Margaret, the baby, was just turned a year. They were so pretty and she was so proud of them. They were the apples of her and their Dad's eyes. It was six months now since he had been called up and had gone into the army, but his letters were full of love for his "four girls", as he called them, and he had spent hours making the shelter comfortable for them. He had made a wooden floor and bunks to sleep on, never really thinking they would need them. How wrong he was! Now his letters were full of worry and he kept urging her to evacuate and take the girls to the country and safety. She had thought about it, but he was only stationed in Kent, with a search-light unit, and he was able to come home on leave now and again. She wanted to be there when he did, but she had promised that if things got too bad she would go.

She knew, of course, that she could always go down into the London Underground or 'Tube', as everyone called it, with her friend and neighbour, Florrie. Every night Flo begged her, "Please Nell, come with me. I worry about you here on your own." But somehow Nell just didn't feel it was safe down there with all those hundreds of people. She told Flo so and wished that Flo and her family would stay in the Anderson with them. But no, Flo would insist on going down the Tube and, of course, it was up to her if she felt safer down there.

Nell gave the girls their cocoa and biscuits and then helped them to use the chamber pot, which she then emptied out into the garden. They said their prayers and settled down for a long and, she hoped, quiet night. She wished that they could have a light but, of course, owing to the blackout, that was impossible. It would be good if she could read a book or write a letter, but as that couldn't be, she had better try to get off to sleep.

She must have dozed off – she didn't know for how long – when the "fireworks" started. She heard a plane and saw the searchlights throwing their long, silver beams across the sky, crossing and crisscrossing in their efforts to catch the "raider" in their sights. Then the bombs rained down. My God, they were close!

"Please God, keep us safe!" She put her arms around the girls to comfort them and started to pray.

"Our Father which art in Heaven..."

Emmie and Marie joined in.

"Thy Kingdom come, Thy will be dome..."

And it will, she thought. *What is to be will be.*

Then, as if in answer to her prayer, it was suddenly quiet. The plane had gone. She hoped they would bring it down on its way back home and wondered what damage it had caused and how many people had been hurt. She calmed down the girls and, cuddling Margaret in her arms, thought, *Please night, hurry up and pass*.

She was just nodding off herself when she heard heavy footsteps on the stone path. Her heart was pumping like a steam-hammer. The steps ceased and she could see the reflection of a torch beam shining around on the far wall. A voice called out, "ARP here. Is anyone there? There is an unexploded bomb in the vicinity and we have to evacuate the area, so please answer if there is anybody there."

She held her breath. What should she do? She didn't recognize the voice. She knew their Warden. It was Maggie O'Connor's dad and he had a beery voice, because he liked a drop or two. No, no, that was no ARP Warden, just some young smart Alec trying it on. She heard him call out once more about the unexploded bomb and the torch was coming nearer. "Please don't look in the shelter," she prayed. Emmie moved and she thought she was going to wake up but, thankfully, she didn't. Nell held her breath and gave a sigh of relief as the footsteps started to go away. Then it was quiet again and she lay there trembling. *Oh, dear God, had she done the right thing? Suppose there was an unexploded bomb?* They were very near and yet they didn't seem to have caused much damage. *Oh, Heaven help us!* No, she was sure she was right. If he had known they were there, they could have been raped, or murdered, or anything. *That settles it*, she thought. Tomorrow she would go round to the school and put their names down for evacuation as soon as possible – and she would go down the Tube with Flo until they did and that was that. Having made up her mind, she sat there, waiting for the dawn and the 'All Clear'.

She must have fallen asleep out of sheer exhaustion. The next thing she knew was that she could hear voices and she looked up. It was daylight. The 'All Clear' must have gone and they'd slept through it. Not surprising really, after the night she'd had. She got up, came out of the shelter and there was Flo, talking to an ARP Warden. Why was Flo crying and the chap comforting her? She waved to them and called out but they didn't seem to hear her. Flo was really upset. Something must have happened down the Tube. That was it! How many times had she told her, begged her not to go down there? But she wouldn't listen. She got up close and thought it strange that they didn't seem to see her and yet they were looking straight at her and what was Flo saying?

"Oh those lovely little girls. If only she had come down the Tube with me. Time and time again I pleaded with her, but she wouldn't. 'Not safe,' she said. Not safe! Gawd, I blame myself, I should have insisted. They would have been alive now if I had.'"

What did Flo mean? And the Warden saying, "They couldn't have known anything about it. They must have been sound asleep because only about fifteen minutes before I went through here, calling out, but nobody answered. You see, this is not my post, it's O'Connor's, but his Missus called in and said he was sick, so I took over. I didn't know they were there. If only I had known, so God help me, I didn't know, I didn't know!"

2. Seaton

The introductory chapter was initially a short story written by my mother when in her mid-seventies, shortly after my father died. Much of the story is fact, not fiction. She wrote it for a competition, which unfortunately she did not win. I am aware of the truth of most of the story as I was five-year-old Marie, which is my middle name. Emmie is my elder sister by two years, whose true name is Patricia or Pat. Margaret is the middle name of my younger sister by four years, Jacqueline or Jackie. It is only the ending of the story that is fictional, most of it being very real.

I have recently learned that the bombing actually took place on 15th October 1940 and an incident which took place on that date but which she omitted from her story is extremely sad and heartrending. However, I need first to relate our family's experiences leading up to the bombing on October 15th.

When the war began, nobody knew what would be happening and most schools arranged for families to be evacuated. Mum, Pat, Jackie and I were evacuated to Seaton in Devon. We were billeted with a charming couple whose large home was usually used as a guesthouse during the summertime. They also ran a market garden, which fascinated me and which I thoroughly enjoyed walking around and exploring with the husband. The house was beautiful and immaculate and Mum was very concerned that we may accidentally cause damage to the home, furniture or even the market garden grounds. She repeatedly advised gently to be quiet and to show respect for the home and garden. Noticing this, the owners were quite concerned for her and asked her if she would feel happier living in 'Pansy Cottage', which they usually hired out during the summer holiday season. Mum gladly accepted their offer and we soon moved in. It was lovely. We had to use oil lamps, candles and an outside loo, but it felt very homely, with a warm fireplace and timber beams. The beach was just around the corner. It was cordoned off with large circles of barbed wire, which we were advised had been placed there in case of enemy invasion. There were soldiers walking up and down the length of the beach, on guard, but we could still walk along the promenade, which we did with great pleasure.

The wife of the owner of 'Pansy Cottage' and the guesthouse had a brother who ran the Job Centre or Labour Exchange, as it was then called, He became aware of Mum's extremely careful thriftiness with the housekeeping money and suggested she might like to visit him at the exchange the following Monday. Mum was very unsure. She had always been a very willing worker but had to consider our welfare. Pat and I were new pupils at the local school, so we were OK, but there were no such things as Day Nurseries or Child Care Centres for babies of Jacqueline's age. But she thought that perhaps he might be able to find her a part-time job and decided to go.

She hopefully visited him on the Monday. She need not have worried as there were very few jobs available out of the summer season, but he dutifully placed her on the dole list, thus allowing her to have dole money. She was absolutely delighted and surprised to receive dole, which meant extra housekeeping money after all the scrimping and scraping during the thirties' depression. Life was happy for us all in Seaton, but it was a very different story for Dad. It was the time of the so-called 'Phoney War'. Nothing was happening; no bombing, no airplanes, just barrage balloons and an occasional practice siren wail. Dad was lonely living on his own and wondering how we were faring. As there was no evidence of the war, he wrote to Mum, asking if she would consider bringing us all home. She responded immediately – our place was at his side so we left happy Seaton and returned to London.

Back in London

I was sad to leave Seaton but in some respects it was good to be together again as a family back in London and at our old school, which was at the end of a short street just opposite our house and Mum could watch us walking to school from an upstairs window. Mum's friend and neighbour (mentioned in her story) 'Auntie Flo' had a daughter, Rene, who was about a year older than Pat and we always walked to school together. Along the way to our left was a small factory with an adjoining house, in which a young couple (who were probably caretakers) lived with their two young children, a boy and a girl. We would stop to join with them and all walk to school together. One day a package of Anderson shelter pieces was delivered, which I believe was arranged by the government for free. Dad soon got to work making the shelter and Pat and I enjoyed watching him. As Mum describes in 'The Warning', he worked meticulously, digging out the deep square base area and then putting the shelter together. He then made the wooden floor, built two sets of double bunks, a staircase of wooden steps leading downwards and a large solid square of wood with a handle each side to place or remove it from either side. When all was finished he made a small garden on the top and covered it with nasturtiums. He said he felt it would be a good disguise from air view and would also make it more attractive. Pat and I were very impressed with it and often played down there if Mum and Dad allowed.

That was before the bombing started...

At first Mum and Dad neatly folded our clothes and laid them at the bottom of our bed, making sure we knew exactly what to do in an emergency, Jackie's clothes were placed beside her cot. If the siren wailed in the middle of the night, one of them would supervise us whilst we dressed ourselves, at the same time they would dress the baby, Jackie. The other went into the kitchen to make a few sandwiches and a flask of hot cocoa. We would then go down the staircase together. Unfortunately, for some unknown reason, one night I sat down on a stair and removed my shoes. Consequently, when walking across the garden to the shelter in the dark, I stood on a three or four inch nail, which entered my heel and I had a very infected heel for some time.

As the bombing was becoming far more threatening and more frequent and at an earlier time, Mum and Dad decided it would be better for us if we went to bed directly to the shelter early in the evening, which Mum clearly describes in

'The Warning'. At about this time the school was arranging a further evacuation and our parents decided that Pat and I should go with the school. Our friend Rene also came with us and Auntie Flo and Mum agreed that we should insist on keeping together.

Exeter

Off we all went on the train, having no idea where it would take us. I suppose it was considered necessary to keep the destination secret. Even the parents had no idea where we were going. We sat on the train with a bar of chocolate, a tin of condensed milk (I have no idea why this was chosen), a luggage label tied to our coat button, a gas mask and a small suitcase holding our belongings. When we arrived in Exeter we were first examined for disease and body mites and our heads examined for lice and then our hair washed. We were then taken to a large hall where we ate a meal. Later we were taken to Exeter market square, in the centre of which we were huddled together into a group. The locals were invited to walk around us and choose which child they would like to billet. As I was then four and Pat was six years old, Mum had requested that we were not to be parted. Nobody wanted three girls and it was decided that Rene would go off alone to a family. In fact, later we learned that she was very happy with the family, but we never saw her again. Pat was adamant that we were not to be parted but no-one felt that they could manage two little girls. We were the last two left and it was beginning to get dark. They just did not know what to do with us until one very kind lady finally agreed to have both of us. She had a tall Victorian town house, which seemed to me to be filled with lots of her own children. We were quite happy there and settled in well with the other children. We did learn that other relatives were fairly near and I do recall that we actually went to see an adult evacuee but I cannot recall who it was. I have discussed this with my mother's youngest sister, Auntie Chris (her real name is Adelaide but she prefers to be called Chris). She reminded me that her father (my grandfather) was quite worried about the effect of the war and bombing on his mother, Great Granny Ward, as she was quite frail and in her late sixties. He asked Adelaide, who was then fifteen years old, if she would accompany great granny Ward and keep an eye on her. He agreed to send her money for her keep. She agreed and they were billeted in a small village outside Exeter, which I believe was called Henvitree. It was probably they whom we visited, but neither I nor Auntie Chris can remember.

Auntie Chris says that they were very happy there. They were staying with a lovely young woman with a small boy. Unfortunately, her husband was in a prisoner of war camp. She used to get lonely and worried, so it was a great joy to have 'Chrissy' and great granny Ward staying with her. However, one day granny went to the local Post Office with her pension book, which still had a few withdrawals in it. She asked if they would arrange for a new book with the London Post Office. However, every week they advised her that it hadn't arrived and she started to worry. Auntie Chris wrote to Grandad, explaining the situation and he agreed to go to the local Post Office and enquire. Meanwhile, he asked her not to worry, as he would send extra money for the pair of them.

The London Post Office was adamant that the book had been sent to grandma's London address. This all caused great stress for great grandma, who was very, very worried (possibly due to her age). One evening she went up to bed early while Auntie Chris stayed chatting to the young mother. Suddenly they heard a thud upstairs and both rushed to see if great grandma was all right. When they got to the bedroom she was lying on the floor. She had fallen out of bed and died. Auntie Chris cannot recall what happened next, but she does remember that Great Granny Ward was taken back to London by train, with the young Auntie Chris organising the journey and watching over the coffin. Grandad had arranged the journey as he actually worked for the railway company. He was distraught and heartbroken. So too was the young mother who had enjoyed Auntie Chris's company so much. Auntie Chris had even done several little jobs for people in the village to add to their income.

Pat and I had heard that someone had died but we didn't realise who it was. I suppose it was thought that we were too young to be told the details. Back in Exeter we just lived a normal life, eating our meals as a family around a large table and going to the park with swings, etc, with the other children. Every night at bedtime Pat and I shared a bed and said our prayers together, as Mum had taught us. Then we kissed 'goodnight' the two photographs she had given us and placed them under our pillows – one of Mum and one of Dad. Mum insisted that we do that each night before going to sleep. Very often 'Uncles' came into the bedroom to sit and talk with us and to wish us 'goodnight'. They were mostly young soldiers who were away from home and family, as we were. They probably felt sympathy for us.

Then, one day, Mum requested that we should be brought back home to London. She had heard from another parent that the house was being run as a brothel. Whether this was true or not, we certainly had suffered no harm. We had just been given kindness and consideration. So back to London we went. Pat was now seven and I was five years old and we joined Mum and Jacqueline once more. Dad was in the army by now. He was 'called up' when he was twenty-six years.

3.   London and Kegworth

As explained in Chapter 2, Mum and Dad had decided that we should go directly to bed in the Anderson shelter, which Mum continued to do when we arrived home from Exeter. This is the point which leads into Mum's story. However, as stated previously, the ending is slightly different. Yes, the bomb did explode, but obviously, we were not killed. We were buried under the rubble and couldn't get out of the shelter via Dad's doorway. He had left a special spanner at the back of the shelter, where there was a planned extra escape route, which had to be unbolted. Unfortunately, the nuts securing the bolts had rusted to them and it was impossible for Mum to remove them. Dad had also left a torch, slightly dimmed by cover, for such an emergency and Pat had to hold the torch whilst Mum tried to unscrew them, but it was impossible. There was nothing to be done but sit amongst the rubble and wait to be rescued. After what seemed an age, help finally arrived and we were dug out and taken to our nearby school, where we stayed the night.

What was extremely sad was that the small factory and house we passed had received a direct hit. Whether that had been the cause of our bomb damage, I have no idea. Our two friends had been sent to live with their grandparents some-where in the country, away from London and so were safe. Their father was in the forces by now so Mum lived in the home alone, probably keeping their job going. She went down to the tube for shelter every night. Unfortunately, their father had come home on leave that day and they had decided to stay together in their own home for the night. Both were killed by the bomb, which was extremely sad for the children, as they had been parted from their parents for some time and would never see them again.

Continuing with our own experience, next day Mum was accompanied back to our bomb-damaged home to collect whatever things she felt were needed, brought them to us and then travelled to the Education Office in Acre Lane, Brixton, to arrange the evacuation of us all. Very sadly, on the way there, the traffic was held up and Mum was horrified to sit watching from the bus as workers were digging out parts of bodies from a shelter in Kennington Park, which must have been bombed the same night as we had been. Mum told us repeatedly that they were so mangled and dismembered that the people were unrecognisable, so the authorities decided to fill in the hole containing the bodies, as there was nothing else they could do.

Mum carried on her journey and it was arranged that we should all be evacuated to Kegworth in Derbyshire, which again is quite a tale, to be explained later.

Mum was certain that there were at least 200 people or more in that shelter and no-one knew who they were or where they came from. She was very cross until she died, aged 91 years, in July 2005, that Lambeth Council had done nothing to commemorate the deaths of those people killed and felt that at least a memorial should have been erected in the park. I urged her to write to Lambeth Council but she didn't. However, when my husband and I decided to move from London in 2006, I decided to write on her behalf. Before starting to write the letter, I happened to glance at the day's London daily paper, and imagine my enormous surprise to read that Lambeth Council had decided to place a memorial in Kennington Park in honour of the hundred or so people who had died there. Mum may have disagreed with the number, but it is such a coincidence after all those years, that I think the psychologist Carl Jung would have called it 'synchronicity' or 'meaningful coincidence'. I am including below some relevant information printed in my retired teachers' association newsletter, offered by Mr Tom Fraser:

"The Kennington Park bomb shelter was, like so many public shelters improvised in parks, just trenches with a thin roof over the top, e.g. corrugated iron. They weren't designed to protect against direct hits, but rather against the blast and debris from near misses. So a direct hit would cause casualties in the trench and the shock wave collapsed part of the trench elsewhere – as happened in Kennington Park on October 15th, 1940. The bomb was probably 'only' a 100kg high explosive weapon. The total of deaths is believed to be 104; accuracy isn't really possible due to the fact that no rosters were kept of people sheltering and many bodies were disintegrated. There is a list of known dead on the Vauxhall and Kennington website. The memorial was unveiled on October 14th 2006."

I have included Mr Fraser's information as I was far too young to understand what happened, but I do know that the 'trench' (shelter) was in a very convenient position quite close to the Oval tube station and several main roads – thus allowing people to swiftly go inside for so-called 'cover'.

The Imperial War Museum has some records of the Kennington Park bombing and were very helpful. Many years ago my husband and I became members and we very often took my mother with us when we visited the museum. As she was elderly, the museum suggested that we telephone them to advise them when we were visiting, having mother with us and they would open the back gates and allow us to park in the grounds so that mother didn't have too far to walk to get inside. When she first saw the list of names of those identified from the Kennington Park shelter, which was on a wall-hung wooden plaque, she was very distressed as some of the named dead, which the authorities had been able to trace, were people she knew, who lived locally. However, she always enjoyed coming to the museum with us as it brought so many memories and also they were so kind to her.

Kegworth

When we arrived in Kegworth we were billeted with two ladies – Mrs Ballard and her thirty-something, unmarried daughter Ethel. I have altered their names for obvious reasons. I assume that they had the most sincere wishes to do something for the 'war effort', as it was called, and to be an example to others to do their part, but they were not really happy about receiving "common London cockneys" and were uncomfortable with our presence. Mind you, there were four of us – Mum, 21-month-old Jacqueline, myself, aged five years and Pat, seven. It seemed they thought all Londoners were cockneys. We were never allowed through the front door and had to enter by the side door straight into the kitchen. In fact, we were allowed only to use the kitchen and the staircase which led to the upstairs bathroom and our bedroom, that is, except on Sundays.

They explained that Mr Ballard, who had died, was a building contractor who had built all the 1930s houses on the estate, selecting the largest corner plot and building the largest and most impressive house for themselves, which, of course, made them superior to everyone around them – at least they thought and implied so.

An arrangement was made with our Mother that she would buy our food shopping and cook our meals, which we would eat in the kitchen; Mrs Ballard and Ethel would provide for themselves and eat separately in the dining room at a different time. Sunday was different, as they professed to be devout worshippers/believers. Pat and I were sent to Sunday School at 10 till 10.30am at the C of E church. Then we would all attend chapel together for the morning service from 11am until 12 noon. We would then have a hurried lunch (in the kitchen, of course) when we returned, as we all had 'jobs' to do. First, we had to roll the old carpet in the hall, which they had laid when they knew we were coming, and put it away in a cupboard, replacing it with the original smart, expensive carpet for the 'worshippers' they were expecting. We then had to enter a very nice room, with French windows, which opened onto the garden, gather chairs and place them in rows, place a hymn book on each chair, wheel out the lectern and a small organ, to prepare for the 2pm home worship service.

To me, as a very young child, it all seemed extremely superficial, both the service and the two ladies. After the service we replaced everything as it had been, sat for a light tea and then all went off to church for Evensong – as Sunday had to be a full day of worship.

It was arranged that Mum would do all the housework, washing and ironing (of course there were no washing machines available in those days) but Mum was not allowed to hang out the washing she had done. Mrs Ballard explained that it would not be correct for the neighbours to see her in the garden and think that they were using her, so Mrs Ballard took out the washing and hung it out. Incidentally, she advised us all that she didn't want us to mix with or talk to any of the neighbours – as it was 'not the correct thing to do'.

Mum was very happy when she received a letter from Dad advising her that he had a few days' leave coming up and wondered whether he would be allowed to stay with us for a while. She enquired from Mrs Ballard if they would find it acceptable and was delighted when they agreed. Everything changed when Dad arrived. They fussed over him and couldn't do enough to please him, even allowing him to enter through the front door. They repeatedly advised us that we should be very grateful that we had such a polite, handsome, well-spoken and intelligent father and husband. This we had to accept with a smile, as Mum had insisted that we were to be polite and grateful to them whatever happened. Some time later, Mum heard that there was a group of Londoners living in town and asked Mrs Ballard if she knew where they lived. She had a horrified, short response from Mrs Ballard.

She must avoid meeting them at all costs as they were not very nice people – they came from the East End of London. However, after much enquiry Mum eventually discovered where they lived. She had probably met them at the Post Office collecting their allowances. Mum had arranged to take us to see them and meet their children.

What a surprise! They were living in a disused slaughter-house. What a place to be billeted in! To me, it appeared to be vast, cold and bare – a huge room with a very high ceiling, which several families shared as a sitting room, but with very little furniture. Presumably, there were other individual family rooms upstairs, which I didn't see or hear of. Pat and I sat on the stone floor and played with the children, probably 'five stones', but it had all been a terrible shock to see people living in such terrible conditions. There appeared to be an atmosphere of death in the room, to me, and I supposed the ceiling was high because the bodies of the dead or waiting to be killed animals were hung there, However, the residents were warm-hearted and cheerful. They were pleased to meet us and welcomed us with a warm cup of tea. It was lovely to see Mum actually smiling happily once more since Dad had left. What an experience and an education for a child of five years.

Then one day we all had a very pleasant surprise. Mum had received a letter from her younger sister, Auntie Rose, advising her that she had managed to get a council house for us in Wolverhampton. Auntie Rose, with Uncle Tom and their young daughter Miriam, had been moved to Wolverhampton from London because Uncle was an engineer and was involved with 'war work'. She suggested that transport could be arranged to collect us. So we said 'goodbye' to Kegworth and the Ballards, never dreaming that we would return within a few months, but, unknowingly, happily moved on to Wolverhampton.

4. Wolverhampton

On arrival in Wolverhampton we moved directly into a large, three-storey council house, on a corner plot facing Bushbury Hill. The house was almost bare as we had very little furniture, which I assume was 'borrowed' from Auntie Rose. We lived in the three rooms on the ground floor, the toilet being just inside the side entrance/back door. There was a kitchen, sitting room (which contained little more than the fireplace, a dining table and four chairs, if I recall correctly. There was also a lovely bay window, with a curtain which ran straight across the front. There was a third room which we used as a bedroom, with a double bed and a chest of drawers, which I vaguely remember. We slept two up and two down in the bed – Mum and Jackie at the top, Pat and I at the bottom. Unfortunately, one night Mum inadvertently kicked her foot forward and I was woken suddenly. Next morning I had a lovely black eye!

For my part, I was very happy at Wolverhampton. There was a sense of freedom and love in the poverty-stricken home. I think it must have been a huge lesson to me that snobbery and middle class 'keeping up with (or even superiority to) the Jones" does not necessarily bring happiness. What a lesson at such a young age! Nevertheless, it has remained with me my whole life and also a deep sense that if GOD represents LOVE then I could feel IT/HIM and know what spirituality really means. Mum was an excellent mother and frequently went without herself to feed and clothe her family.

In the mornings Pat and I walked up the lovely Bushbury Hill opposite our house to the country lane in which our primary school was situated. It was the happiest school I have ever attended, largely due to the presence of the head-mistress – a kind, sophisticated and charming middle-aged lady, whom I adored. I believe her name may have been Miss Guerney. In fact, from that experience I have always considered that the Headteacher created the ambience of any school. Miss Guerney took us on many walks along the country lanes, pointing out and naming the trees, the pussy willows, catkins and all manner of wild flowers. I was enthralled by the peace, beauty and the earthy spirituality of the countryside.

When there was snow, Pat and I dragged a sledge up the hill. I have absolutely no idea where it came from, unless mother had arranged something for us. On the way home from school we slid all the way down the hill on the sled. What great joy!

At home we were bathed in the huge kitchen sink, as Mum kept the door in the sitting room, which led upstairs to the bathroom, firmly locked. We had no light bulbs up there, nor carpeting or linoleum, just wooden staircases and floors, so there was no need for us to have access. The curtained bay window made an ideal space for a small stage and at weekends we would give little shows to Mum and Auntie Rose, singing and dancing, reciting poetry and performing short 'plays' which we had written ourselves, dressing up with whatever clothes and materials we could find.

Mum was excellent in finding odd bits and pieces of material or old clothing. As everything was rationed, one needed coupons to buy anything. I really do not know how she did it but one day we came home from school to find her with some material and old clothing, a piece of sacking (originally a potato sack) and three crochet hook type needles. She explained that between us we should be able to make a small rug for the floor, which would be very handy. She showed us how to do it, which was quite simple really. She took a piece of material and cut it into an oblong roughly 3mm wide and 10mm long. She then took one of the hooked needles, with which she pushed one end of the material into a hole in the sacking and then hooked it back up into and through the next hole. It was so simple but so effective. At first we started to cut the material. Mum may have possibly managed to obtain two pairs of scissors, probably borrowed.

Then we all sat together, 'crocheting' the odd pieces of material. Mum sat at one end of the sacking and Pat and I each worked at a corner at the opposite end. It was great fun working together. Of course Jackie was far too young and probably slept whilst we worked. It was good to see the rug slowly developing from our work and when it was finished we were quite pleased with the result. The rug proved to be very hard wearing but I have absolutely no idea what happened to it when the war was over. It possibly lasted for years.

Another thing Mum encouraged was for us to join the library and some nights we would sit quietly reading. Mum, all her life, was very committed to education. She felt it was imperative for one to gain knowledge of the world and life in general, thus perhaps helping to prevent further wars, as she had lost an uncle in the First World War and Dad's father was gassed and released in 1917 and died two years later from gas poisoning.

One dark, rainy evening we were all sitting at the table reading our library books, when quite suddenly we heard heavy, plodding male footsteps from the front door straight up the bare wooden staircase. We were very frightened as the front door was always locked and bolted top and bottom. Mum found our torch and the key to unlock the sitting room door. We all huddled together for safety. Imagine our amazement when we saw large, wet footprints all the way up the stairs, but the front door was locked and bolted as usual. There was nothing for it but for all of us to go up the stairs with our torch and search the two upper floors.

The footprints stopped at the top of the stairs on the first floor. We looked in and around the bathroom and the other two rooms, searching cupboards as we went – but there was nothing. We then carried on up to the next floor, although there were no footprints up there. We found no sign of anyone in any room, nor any further footprints. We huddled together down the stairs, knowing full well that we had clearly heard the footsteps and observed the wet footprints. We never mentioned it again as it seemed to be something we should all forget.

Mum carefully locked the sitting room door as she had always done. We learned many years later that for Mum she felt it was the unluckiest house she had ever lived in. We had only been there for a short while when somebody stole all the coal from the coal bunker in the garden. Of course there was no heating in the house except the coal fire in the sitting room and the cooker in the kitchen, where Mum bathed us in the deep earthenware sink. Mum had very little money. Dad's hard earned savings, plus that which Mum had also earned and saved slowly diminished and she had not received her army allowance. The Post Office knew nothing about her as Kegworth Post Office had not arranged to transfer it to Wolverhampton, as Mum had requested.

Next, someone broke in and stole the money from the meters. Mum had not noticed it until the police came with a young man who had robbed the meters in the whole street and had informed the police that he had robbed our meters, when he was caught. Mum had to find the money to repay the Gas and Electric Boards.

Finally, Mum had run out of money. It had been snowing heavily and was very cold. She placed her last half-crown (two shillings and sixpence i.e. twelve and a half pence) in a small purse, gave it to us with our ration books and sent us, with one of our local girlfriends, to get some stewing steak, with which she had intended to make a stew and a pie and eke them out to feed us all for a few days.

Pat was a very sensible, mature girl for her age, a real surrogate mother, but when we reached the butchers, imagine Pat's surprise and horror when she discovered that the half--crown coin had disappeared from the purse. We walked backwards and forwards, searching everywhere in the snow for the lost half-crown, but just couldn't find it.

When we arrived home and confessed to Mum she didn't scold us as expected but worse, she just sat and cried and we joined her. We knew how important it had been and the three of us sat crying and hugging each other.

It was then that Mum decided that she would have to re-turn to London to find out what had happened to her army pay allowance, plus the extra few shillings Dad had added to it from his own very meagre army pay. She also needed to arrange for some housing, as we had left our bomb-damaged, rented flat so suddenly. I've no idea who paid for it, but Pat and I were driven back to Kegworth and the ladies Ballard and Mum kissed us goodbye and she and Jackie made their way back to London.

5.   Back to Kegworth

I often wonder why on earth Mrs Ballard and her daughter agreed to billet Pat and I without Mum accompanying us. It must have been a handful for the mother as she was an elderly lady (or so she seemed to me) and her daughter was at work all day. I've no idea what sort of work she did. It was not considered correct for us to ask such personal questions. I can only consider that Pat and I couldn't have been such bad children if they were willing to accept us again. Although, of course, they did receive a billeting allowance, which may have been of financial assistance to them. I've really no idea unless the local authority insisted on their billeting someone. Nor do I know how the agreement and arrangements were made for our return.

Very few people had house telephones in those days and, of course, there were no such things as mobile telephones. We, as children, never questioned the decisions of our parents. Usually, we just did as we were told. How different from today's society! Letter writing was the main communication technique. In an emergency a telegram would be sent via the Post Office and delivered by a very smartly dressed young man in uniform, on a bicycle, with a small box attached to a leather strap, which he wore over his shoulder and across his chest. He also wore a smart 'pill-box' hat. If one saw a telegram boy approaching the house one faced him with fear and dread. Mostly it was used to send bad news, very often of the death of someone – especially of a dear one killed in the forces.

My memories of this time are scant. Perhaps I deliberately wiped some things from my mind. However, I do remember some incidents, both good and bad. Pat and I walked to school, which was probably a mile or so away. I know that at that time I frequently suffered from stomach upsets and unfortunately one day I was taken short on the way home from school. Pat, being a very caring, loving and protective elder sister (and sometimes a little bossy), ushered me into the nearby churchyard to relieve myself.

Unfortunately, the situation was made very inconvenient (pardon the expression) because during the winter months Mum clothed us in 'combs" (an abbreviation of the word 'combinations'), being a single garment of combined vest and underpants, made from soft, warm woollen material; a very good idea but very difficult to unbutton in an emergency. Needless to say, I had an unfortunate accident and was very, very distressed. Pat and I had to go home to face Mrs Ballard, who was absolutely furious. We were sent straight up to the bathroom and Pat had to assist in washing me down. We had to remove the "combs' which Pat had then to wash and wash until any stains had been removed, which really was an almost impossible task. Meantime, I had to re-dress and present myself to Mrs Ballard, who took me straight to the garden wood shed and locked me in for the night without food or drink, in the dark and amongst spiders, cobwebs, beetles, etc. I was lonely, cold, frightened and hungry and mostly I missed my mum, coupled with an enormous sense of guilt.

A much more pleasant recollection is of some friends we made at school, who lived nearby but on a small council estate. We were forbidden to mix with them but they were very friendly and urged us to go home with them without Mrs Ballard knowing and after school one day we agreed, feeling very conscious of breaking the rules. When we entered the house we were welcomed by both their mother and their father. The house was filled with children of all ages, with a toddler on the floor and a baby in mum's arms. Dad was sitting in an armchair. It appeared that he couldn't work as he had injured his back at work some years before, but the house was filled with joy and love. Mum was a real 'earth mother' and immediately made a pot of tea, with the baby in her arms. They had few cups, but the children drank from wide-necked half pint milk bottles. Pat and I were honoured with a mug each. The children had thick slices of bread and jam for tea, which we politely refused, explaining that Mrs Ballard would be expecting us. They were obviously very poor but Dad had us all laughing, telling us stories and witty jokes. On consideration, I think they felt sorry for us, yet they had so little themselves.

After that day, we often arranged to meet our friends without Mrs Ballard's knowledge. They took us to some wonderful country places, not far away, which we would never have seen. The two Ballard ladies did what they felt was the best for us but the nearest to this was a walk along a very long country lane after Evensong on Sundays. Sadly it was extremely boring for two young children as there were tall hedges each side and nothing else but the occasional wooden post with metal rungs at the side, which I realize now were telegraph posts. After a short while we would turn round and return home. I suppose they felt that we ought to have some fresh air or exercise and also they needed to keep us occupied. If it was raining, or not suitable to go out then we were made to sit and write to our Mother under their jurisdiction.

How different the outings with our friends were. They would take us to a beautiful meadow nearby, which was absolutely covered with wild flowers such as poppies, buttercups and daisies, cornflowers, cow parsley, meadowsweet and many others. Cornflowers became my favourite flower and still remain special to me. Sadly they are now very hard to find. During the war the fields were left to go fallow for a year on rotation, which I assume was a long tradition. Today's farming is very different, with not just one harvest but two or even three in one season in one field being yielded. In one nearby meadow there was an ancient, large broken down wooden houseboat docked in an old, dried-up stream. What stories we invented acting as pirates, sailors, war heroes etc – so good for starved imaginations.

They taught us how to make daisy chains, use a buttercup under the chin to discover if you had a liking for butter (completely naive of course) also how to be rid of warts by using the milk from dandelion stalks. We used dock leaves to rub away the irritation caused by stinging nettles. All quite an education really, given by poor "ignorant council tenants".

One day, when Pat and I came home from school, we were met by a stony-faced 'Auntie' Ethel, who was waiting for us just inside the kitchen doorway. She told us to follow her upstairs, which we immediately obeyed, not knowing why.

Eventually, we entered a huge, very smart bedroom, which we had never seen before. Mrs Ballard was lying in a large double bed, with a gentleman sitting by her bedside. Another, strange-looking, gentleman was sitting across the room by the window. The gentleman beside the bed explained that he was a doctor and gestured for us to go towards him. He stated that Mrs Ballard was very ill with pneumonia and bronchitis and because of us she was being taken to hospital. If she died it would be our fault, we would have killed her. Therefore, the other gentleman, a Mr Wall, would be taking us away. I was terrified! Mr Wall had what is known as a 'wall eye' – his right eye was misshapen and lay at the top of its socket. He looked formidable and very threatening to me, as a young child, and I thought he was evil and was sent to chastise us for our bad behaviour.

Nothing could have been further from the truth. We eventually discovered that he was a very kind country peasant – a working man with a gentle heart. He worked as a car mechanic in a local garage, we learned later. He took us home to a most delightful old country cottage, roughly between 200 to 300 years old, which surely would be regarded as unhealthy and be demolished today. His elderly wife was anxiously awaiting us there, We never saw the Ballards again, although when we visited Kegworth many, many years after the war, we saw both of their graves in the aforementioned churchyard and it was quite clear that they both lived for many years after the war.

When we entered the home of Mr and Mrs Wall – dear 'Auntie' and 'Uncle' – it was as if time had stood still. We entered a much more rural way of living in which we instinctively felt relaxed and 'at home'. It felt we were living much closer to reality in a culture which perhaps had barely changed for centuries. The entrance door was at the side of the house, with a short garden path that wound round to the door. There was a small window each side of the door, which led directly into the sitting/dining room, with a dining table to the left beneath the window. On the right-hand side was a wall with a door in the middle, which led into the rarely used drawing room.

What was most interesting was a small cupboard in the near left corner of the room which, when opened was not truly what it seemed, as there was a secret panel which, when moved, revealed a small, winding staircase leading upstairs to a very similar cupboard, also with a secret panel. The door to the cupboard entered a very large bedroom containing a huge, ancient four-poster bed. Mrs Wall explained that this was what was once called a 'priest hole'. It probably dated back to the 1600s and the Civil War.

The Walls' grandma remained in that bed day and night as long as we were there. She must have been mainly sleeping as we never saw her awake, but we did hear on occasion the banging of her stick on the floor to gain attention. I assume that 'Auntie' washed and dressed 'Grandma' when we were out or at school. At the side of her four-poster there was a small bedside cabinet on top of which were Grandma's water, medicine, pills, etc, some of which were sulphur tablets. We must have experienced them before for me to know what they were. Pat loved them but I didn't like them at all. Sometimes we would crawl around the four-poster on our knees and Pat would raise her arm and take a few sulphur tablets, which had an unfortunate flatulence effect on her digestion. She enjoyed them as sweets, which were rationed and thus we had them on very rare occasions. I don't think that Grandma knew anything regarding our antics.

Downstairs there was a large fireplace opposite the drawing room and in between the two walls connecting them was a wall with the door to the kitchen, which was very ancient with a stone floor. A doorway from there led to an outhouse, which contained the ancient stone copper, beneath which a fire would be lit to boil the water placed inside ready for the washing. The copper had a round wooden lid with a handle to lift it. The 'dolly" – a small wooden pole with crossed handles at the top and bottom, would be twirled around and pumped up and down to swirl and clean the washing. There was also a large iron mangle with wooden rollers and an iron turning handle. When turned, the mangle would squeeze out the water from the washed articles. Pat and I would take turns to be responsible either for the turning of the dolly or the mangle handle – such homely, earthy fun, filled with love and happiness. The outhouse had no outer wall and was open to the garden on one side. It was so large that the washing could be hung beneath the roof in inclement weather.

In the garden was an old, gnarled apple tree which, we were told, was over 200 years old. I didn't know that apple trees lived that long but I do know that it produced a copious harvest of delicious apples. To the left of the garden there were rabbits kept in hutches for extra meat rations (though we never observed one being killed) and to make articles of clothing such as hats and gloves for extra income. There was an 'eternal' feeling, as though life had continued in this earthy atmosphere for hundreds of years, so far from the noise, killing and destruction of London, perhaps inspiring my love for the 'natural' and also Shakespeare's 'earthy' plays.

Back inside the cottage, in the far corner of the sitting room, between the kitchen wall and the drawing room wall, was a large, winding staircase, which led directly into Auntie and Uncle's large bedroom. There was no door. Grandma's bedroom was to the left, which did have a door.

Pat and I had to walk to the right across their room to a small 'attic' room, with a door, which was our room. It was obviously used as a storeroom, as there were trays of apples and vegetables from the garden stored for the winter. Our bed was to the right of the room beneath the sloping roof. There was a tiny window up high on the wall to the left of our bed and I could lie there at night looking up at the most beautiful starry sky (there was no light pollution in those days). Mum had taught us that she and Dad, though far away, were beneath the same sky, which comfortingly seemed to bring them closer. At times I felt a certain connection, as if we all were a part of the whole Universe – planets, stars etc – all one being.

We were quite naughty sometimes at night, as we felt so far removed from the rest of the house that we would walk around our attic bedroom and probably play – I have no actual idea what we did, but Mr Wall would sometimes come up and tell us to go to sleep. Rather cheekily, we would play a game where one of us would say, quite suddenly, "There's Mr Wall" and we would judge how quickly we could rush and jump into bed. We took turns to say this. One night we were caught out. Uncle was there behind the door and his voice boomed out, "Yes, Mr Wall is here and I want you to get to bed!" After that shock we felt rather sheepish and guilty and tried hard to be more quiet and better behaved.

On Sundays, after morning church, we would come home with Auntie to prepare lunch and Uncle would pop off to the local to meet friends and family. He didn't stay there long, but obviously had had a little drink and returned home in a very kind and loving mood. He would sit at the dining table beside the window and place one of us on each knee, saying something similar to, "You know that uncle loves you and wouldn't harm you, but I do ask you to try to be good girls and then I wouldn't have to chastise you, would I?" We would look down in embarrassment and promise to try, which we really did, as Auntie and Uncle were so kind.

We never observed Mr Wall having time off from work except on Sundays, but one time when we came home from school he was in the sitting/dining room with his arm in a sling, looking very pale and tired. Auntie explained that he had been taken to hospital because he had had an accident at work and had broken his arm. Apparently, he was using a crank handle to start the engine of a van, when it suddenly kicked back and broke his arm badly. Cranks were often used in those days to start cars; they were an iron handle which was placed into a small hole beneath the radiator. They were very dangerous to use, as they often swung back and could cause serious injury.

Mr Wall went back to work the following day, with his arm in a sling and had no further time off. In those days it was highly unlikely that one would be paid when taking time off, for whatever reason. It must have been difficult for him to work. I can't imagine how he managed. Of course, there was no such thing as the Welfare State or the National Health Service in those days and sick pay just didn't exist. I remember when we went back to live in London Mum had to pay into a special fund which the doctor operated, so that, if any one of us was sick he deducted his fee from the fund.

Mrs Wall was a homely, practical lady, who always encouraged us to assist her when she was making things or just generally working. That is, except on Saturdays, when she went to buy the weekly shopping. Of course, there were no supermarkets or the like then. She would visit the butchers, the grocery shop, the bakers and the greengrocers individually.

I can recall one shop (maybe the Co-op or a haberdashery shop) which had a small round pot-shaped object connected to a wire, which the shop assistant would pull down and unscrew, placing the bill and the money inside, then screw back the lid and direct it on the wire to the cashier, who was sitting high up in a tiny box-like room. The cashier then replaced the contents with either the change and receipt or just the receipt and sent it back to the assistant.

It would have been difficult for 'Auntie' to take us with her and keep an eye on us, so she always ensured that we were kept busy. She would supply us with shopping catalogues, scissors, paper and paste and colouring pencils. We would sit contented for any length of time, cutting out and pasting anything that caught our eyes. Today I suppose it would be called a collage, but at that time we just thought we were making pretty pictures. Sometimes we would cut out a posing model and fit different clothes, which we had cut out, on her to make her look more attractive, we thought.

One day, sometime in October 1941, a young soldier came to see us. It was our real Uncle Jack, who had been stationed not too far away in Osmaston. Uncle Jack had married Kitty, one of Dad's sisters. Earlier, in London, when I was three and Pat was five, they were courting teenagers and would take us every Sunday afternoon to Sunday School. They had married in the early war years. Auntie Kitty was a wonderful seamstress and had scraped up the material somehow, to enable her to make two bridesmaids' dresses and her own wedding dress. Unfortunately, the photographer's shop was bombed the night after the wedding and all the photographs were destroyed. They had to go to another photographer in their wedding outfit on another day and so ended up with one photograph of just those two. A typical wartime incident.

Apparently Uncle Jack was homesick. He hadn't been married long and at age 20 years he missed his wife. When he heard we were not too far away he agreed with Mum, who was very concerned to know where we were billeted and with whom (although she and the Walls always kept in touch by post) to visit us and let her know how we were and the conditions of our billet. He wrote to her later, telling her how we had adapted and how happy we were. He was so impressed by his "lovely little girls" and the way we had settled, with no tears or complaints, that it taught him a great lesson. He learned to 'get on with things' without complaint and shoulder his responsibilities.

Two months later, in December, another very handsome and loving young man in his uniform came to see us. It was our darling Dad! He had come to take us home, back to London, where we could all spend Christmas together. What a lovely surprise! We thanked Mr and Mrs Wall, who hurriedly packed up the Christmas presents which Mum had sent for us, and said 'Goodbye'.

My grandfather, who discovered me washing my hands and face in a bowl at the kitchen sink and chided me for using too much water. During the war, the government decreed that we should save water and when bathing only 4 inches depth of water should be used in the bathtub.

Pat (left) and I, which Mum probably had taken
before we were evacuated with the school.

Dad, soon after he went into the Army at 26 years of age
(when Pat and I were in Exeter).

Mum's younger sister Rose, who arranged for us to
go to Wolverhampton to be near her.

On the bottom front left is Auntie Rose, before she married and moved to Wolverhampton. Bottom right is Adelaide (Auntie Chris), having returned from Devon. At the back is Uncle John, just returned from evacuation in Dorchester. Back in London, he immediately enlisted in the Air Training Corps, where he met my future husband, Peter, newly-arrived from Berkshire and also an ATC cadet. Neither of the young men actually served in the Royal Air Force. John was placed in the Royal Navy and Peter was 'called up' into the Army.

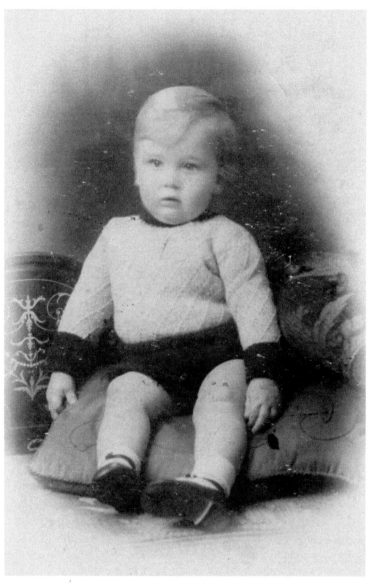

On the back of this photograph Mum had written:
'To Daddy, with love from Albert Jr XXX'
She had obviously sent it to Dad.

Mum holding one of the boys, possibly Bob, in early 1945. The young man behind her lived in the flat which has the front door showing. His father was a sergeant in the Middle East and his mother worked all day. He and his three sisters were with our family much of the time.

1/1584893. Dvr. Lemmer. A.E.
Wed's 11th
551 (GT) Coy RASC
April
A Platoon
B.L.A.

My Darling Wife
Just the usual few lines to let
you know I am fit and well. I'm so sorry
I havent been able to write for these
last few days, but I hope you havent
been worried. I recieved two letters from
you yesterday and one from my Ma, but
its not your fault. I havent recieved your
mail and neither is it my fault that
I havent been able to write before,
for you see. I am on detachment now, and
that means I'm all over the place also that
I only get your mail when I'm back, and
same applies to my mail to you, I can
only send it through my own unit. Thanks
for the photo's of Sheila and Sonny, they
are both lovely, infact Sheila looks very
sweet, it's a pity Pat and Jackie moved.
You are quite right, I am glad you are
back home at last. I'm glad you are

The letter which Dad sent to Mum on 11th April 1945, showing how positive he
was at the time, so different from when he was demobbed in 1946 (February),
almost a broken man.

My mother arranged for two coats to be made from a grey blanket for Pat and I when we were in Wolverhampton. This made a saving on clothing coupons.

Dad on convalescence.

Mum's two brothers Bob (Army) and John (Navy) in Singapore when the RASC allowed uncle Bob to travel from Burma to meet his brother.

Jacqueline probably at the end of the war. She was always unwell when dad returned to the Army after leave because she was pining for him.

My mother and father dancing at the wedding of their granddaughter Tracey,
Jackie's eldest daughter. Sadly, Tracey died with multiple tumours on the brain
within a year. This broke father's heart and he also died within a few months, of
a heart attack. Shortly after his death, mother wrote The Warning, possibly
remembering the early years of their marriage.

A recent photo of me – Sheila Lemmer Dobson.

The Green Man, who appeared personally to me and encouraged my further investigation into the meaning.

Another image of The Green Man, drawn by my husband.

6. London

It was very exciting for Pat and I to travel to our new home in London with our Dad and become a family once more. Of course, it was dark when the huge steam train came puffing into the station. It had slam doors and a long corridor, which was filled with soldiers armed with kitbags, upon which some were sitting and others lying, but all seemed rather sleepy. One soldier was even sleeping in the luggage rack in one of the compartments. I believe the compartments had four seats each side, facing each other, with a sliding door into the corridor and a slam door on the opposite side, all made with beautiful solid, smooth wood.

There were lights in the compartments and the corridor, but they were all kept very dim and all the windows and doors with upper windows were covered with dark blinds, pulled down because of the blackout. Dad kept us occupied by suggesting that we count the number of miles we were travelling according to the rhythm of the train wheels - e.g. 101, 102, etc. He completely fooled us, but it kept us concentrating until we too fell asleep.

On our arrival at London there was a hive of activity. There were men in uniforms everywhere and so many different uniforms! Not only were there army, navy and air force, but I learned later that there were Czechs, French, Polish, Australians, New Zealanders, Dutch, Canadians and Americans and probably others. Dad led us to the Underground (another new and exciting experience for us). Again, the train was filled with soldiers. It was all so busy and full of activity, so different from our life in Kegworth. When we arrived at our destination – the Oval Station – it was completely different once more. The first thing we saw was the bomb-damaged St Mark's Church, probably caused by the Kennington Park shelter bombing. Little did I know that I would be married in that church thirteen years later. As we left the Oval Station we walked into a mystical stillness, no street lights, house lights or traffic to be seen or heard, but a wonderful moonlight which filled the sky (I'm almost sure that it was a full moon), coupled with brilliant twinkling stars, with white fluffy clouds floating by. It was magical for a child! Much to our amazement, they were accompanied by a large barrage balloon.

We turned left and soon began to walk alongside a high wall, which I discovered later, was part of the vicarage garden of St Mark's Church, the vicar being Revd Montgomery, uncle to General Montgomery, who had been born there in the lovely old house, to which in the future we would be invited to many garden fêtes. Next to the house and garden was a small parish hall, beautifully furnished. It was called Tramway Hall, obviously due to the passing traffic, mostly trams, which travelled between Victoria and Camberwell and beyond. Again, I was unaware that I would be confirmed in Tramway Hall, which had to be used as the church for many years until St Mark's was restored. Thus it was, of course, furnished as a church. There was also a hut in the garden grounds, which I learned later when I became a guide. The hut was used as the parish hall.

Opposite Tramway Hall was the Oval cricket ground, which had been taken over by the army. There were sandbags covering every window and spare space. I believe there was a large Bofors gun in the grounds, which terrified me at night during air raids, with its loud explosions, alongside the drone of aircraft and the loud explosions when bombs fell. It was said that a German pilot had been forced to bale out of his damaged aircraft and actually landed in the Oval grounds with his parachute. It was also said that many local women collected together, carrying brooms, hammers, sticks and anything with which to beat the airman and that the soldiers surrounded him and hurried him to a waiting army vehicle to take him from harm's way. As I saw none of this myself, I have no idea of the validity of the story, but it was exactly the type of wartime anger and hysteria felt by many of the women, true or untrue.

As we continued the beautiful moonlit walk to our new home, which our Mother had worked so hard to get for us after the Kennington bombing, we passed through some large, ornate iron gates and fence railings running into Meadow Road, which obviously had once been a real meadow. We turned right and again entered some large, impressive gates just as a nearby clock started to strike twelve midnight. It was so impressive and added to the air of magic for me! In actual fact, we learned that the clock belonged to the French convent next door, the grounds of which, I was told, had once extended as far as the Thames at Vauxhall. In fact, the council estate had been built on part of the convent grounds and was newly-built. From the upper floors of the flats one could clearly see the French nuns/nurses in striking uniforms hurrying about their duties along an outer corridor. What was left of the gardens and grounds was very pretty and attractive with palm trees. The council estate grounds had a long line of fruit trees – apple, pear etc, which must have originally belonged to the convent. Sadly, the fine iron gates and railings of the council estate were later taken away for the war effort, along with millions of pots and pans, which had been requested and which people had willingly contributed for the 'war effort' – only to discover that they were of the wrong type of metal and not used!

On the stroke of twelve midnight we knocked on our new door, which was immediately opened throwing out a vivid beam of electric light, with a lady standing there whispering, "Quick, come in because of the blackout." She gave us such a lovely hug each that I knew instantly, "this is our Mum."

She then told us that she had a lovely Christmas surprise for us. It was our new sixteen-day-old brother! Jacqueline was not around. Mum explained that because of the war expectant mothers were made to travel into the country to give birth, as it was too dangerous in London hospitals. Mum had been forced to place Jackie into care, whilst she, herself, was sent to Oxford, but assured us that she and Dad (who was on compassionate leave for the birth of his son), were doing all that they could to have Jackie back for Christmas in four days' time. Sadly, they had a very difficult time. The authorities just kept explaining that Jackie was too ill to be sent home. In spite of Mum's weekly pestering and hounding, Jackie was not released until the following March and there was nothing that either Mum or Dad could do about it. We didn't even know where she was, due to 'war secrecy'. Mum had tenaciously tried everything. Today we hear of the fate of many children who were placed into care for whatever reason. The authorities regarded them as 'neglected' or orphaned children and had them shipped off to Australia for the rest of their lives, without the parents' knowledge or assent and neither would meet ever again. Thank God Mum and Dad had been persistent and managed eventually to secure Jackie's return to us.

We settled down to our new life in a council flat and went to yet another new school, which of course, was sandbagged around the ground floor, particularly the windows, the upper floor windows being criss-cross taped. At first I went into the beginners class, but soon moved up to the next class. What I remember most about this class was that the teacher was very fond of crochet and would sit crocheting while we chanted out our times tables, or took turns to read aloud, or to sit writing a story. She used to make small circular rings to fit over jam or honey pots and would sew beads at certain points around the edges, to give them weight. I am amazed when I think of the commitment and excellent behaviour of the children in those days!

We were very fortunate to have a flat in the new estate as there were swings, roundabouts and a slide in the grounds so we could easily play nearby without Mum worrying, during the day time, but it was the night times that tired us out, with the guns and bombing. The A.R.P. wardens would come around and call, "Put that light out!" if they saw even a chink of light and often, in the morning we would go outside and see buckets turned upside down, covering incendiary bombs that had been covered with sand to 'put them out'.

As the flats were opposite the Oval cricket grounds, they were all named after cricketers. Our block was called Wisden House. What I remember most was the lovely community spirit there. Most families, like ourselves, had been bombed out of their homes but everyone seemed to accept the dangerous and difficult lifestyle with great courage and fortitude. Some families had lost their father through the war. My best friend, June Cullingford, and her two sisters and brother were being raised by their mother, as their father had been killed whilst on duty as an air raid warden. Most flats held mothers with families because their husbands were away with the services. I never heard anyone complaining of their lot, even those who had lost fathers and husbands. The women were marvellous at holding things together.

Mum told us that when she went to her regular post office to enquire regarding her allowance, the female staff were so relieved and happy to learn that we were all still alive. They had thought that we had all been killed, probably having been bombed, but they refused to advise the Authorities just in case we were still alive and they had saved all the weekly allowances Mum should have received. It was a great relief for both Mum and the staff. Of course, Mum had to repay all the money she had been given to cover the cost of our and her fares and for her housekeeping.

Rationing was very difficult, but Mum was a very efficient housewife and was able to make a healthy meal from whatever was available. The thirties' depression had been a good lesson, especially as, being the eldest, Mum had had to raise her own two brothers and sisters without her mother. My father also took on the family when he married her. We children went without very little. Each morning we would line up and Mum would slice about a quarter of an inch of Mars bar for each of us and that was our sweet ration for the day. We were delighted to receive it and thought we were privileged. Such fruit as oranges, lemons and bananas, etc were very, very scarce. Should a local greengrocer happen to receive a delivery of fruit, one of the neighbours would rush to advise Mum and she would send us off to stand in the long queue with one ration book each. We were only allowed to receive one piece of fruit per person with one ration book only, for whatever fruit had arrived. We all regarded it as a luxury brought to us by the courage of the merchant seamen.

Mum's cousin, Auntie Eileen, nicknamed 'Dinkie', who lived nearby, had married a Canadian fighter pilot officer and they regularly came to visit us. He loved the family atmosphere and very often brought some of his Canadian colleagues when they were off duty. They were very happy being with us until the regular night-time siren warning sounded and the bombs started to drop, the guns booming and the planes droning, then they would become very restless and anxious. They were amazed at the way in which we accepted it all. They explained that they would sooner be up in the air in their planes. It was their job to fight off the enemy and could not understand how we had learned to live with the danger and the constant "thud' of the guns, plus the loud explosions. If the 'All Clear' siren went off they then settled down and would play one of our various games with us once more.

The VI Rockets or "Doodlebugs' or 'Buzz Bombs', as we called them, created an extremely different situation, quite new and unnerving. They arrived at any time, day or night, without any warning. They actually passed over the council flat grounds (the "squares') and we would stand and watch them fly over, with their droning sound and the flames roaring out of the back-end. One could hear the drone of the doodlebug as it thundered along, but then it suddenly went silent as it fell, until there was a loud explosion when it hit the ground or some building. This was very worrying at night-time.

Mum decided to explore the brick shelters that had been erected opposite our flat. There were two long oblong build-ings attached back to back. To enter one went down about half a dozen steps and entered a door on the right. One was immediately confronted by a square of curtaining, door height, with one curtain dividing it into two sections. Each had a metal bucket for toilet facilities, with just the curtain between them. Along each wall were two-tier bunks with probably (if I remember properly) about six feet of distance between the outer walls.

There was an unpleasant smell of dampness and Mum decided that it was not the correct place for us to sleep, although both shelters were always filled with residents every night. Mum decided to clear one bedroom, which appeared to have an outer wall which was reinforced and looked quite strong. She placed our very durable, square dining table in one corner of the room and made up one huge bed on the floor. Should any of us feel anxious when hearing the drone of the doodlebugs we could all squeeze together under the table – Mum, Pat, myself, Jackie and toddler Albert-Anthony. Mum would tell us all to pray for safety when the droning stopped and as soon as the rocket had exploded she would ask that we all pray for the poor souls that it had fallen on. It was a very sad time for everyone.

On a brighter note, I have a wonderful recollection of arriving home from school in the afternoon, entering into a delightful smell of cooking – jam roly-poly pudding, custard tart, spotted dick, bread pudding, bread and butter pudding, stews, meat pies or puddings, casseroles, cakes and all manner of meals. We even had, at times, rice pudding or semolina pudding. How on earth Mum managed to secure the ingredients I do not know. She was a wonderful cook and the way she managed to stretch our meagre rations to produce such food was miraculous. She had four children's ration books, plus her own and she used them sensibly.

When one walked from the entrance hall into the sitting room, the eye was immediately taken by the large, shiny black coal-fired range, with a glistening black kettle steaming on top and a small oven at the side in which we sometimes cooked jacket potatoes. Mum had a very long-handled fork on which she would place a slice of bread and make toast for each of us in turn. On very special occasions she would place a marshmallow sweet and toast one for each of us.

One Wednesday, Uncle Tom arrived from Wolverhampton. Auntie Rose could not bear to think of us suffering with the continuous bombing, especially the doodlebugs, and wanted us to go back to Wolverhampton with him. Mum was not really keen, but she agreed to allow him to take Jackie and I. Arrangements had to be made at the education offices in Acre Lane, Brixton, and off we went immediately.

Mum had been hoping to stay at home with Pat and toddler Albert. Unfortunately it was not to be, due to the introduction of the new V2 rockets – far worse than the original VIs. The following Sunday lunchtime a V2 exploded on Stoddart House, which overlooked the Oval cricket ground, causing absolute devastation. Half of Stoddart House was demolished and the debris was strewn all over Harleyford Road. All the windows of the surrounding blocks of flats, including Wisden House, were blown in and the curtains destroyed. Mum went to investigate a little later and discovered that several people had been killed, including a young mother and her new-born baby. This made Mum very anxious, as she now had an added responsibility. She was expecting another child. She felt it her duty to save her children, so she, Pat and Albert travelled to Wolverhampton to join us.

The reason why Mum went to investigate the bombing of Stoddart House was that she had no idea what had caused the enormous explosion that Sunday lunchtime. The V2 rocket made no sound at all until it had fallen and hit its target and, of course, there was no warning siren. One may imagine the shock everyone felt when the explosion took place as it was so unexpected. When Mum arrived at the bomb site she was quite surprised to see one of her uncles there. (I believe it was one of her Mother's brothers). He was with the WVS (now called the WRVS – Women's Royal Voluntary Service). She was so taken aback that she questioned what he was doing there. He explained that he always helped the WVS because they did such a wonderful job. They visited anywhere where there was a disaster or devastation, supplying comfort, sandwiches and mostly, a cup of hot tea, to calm those affected, which is exactly what he did for Mum. He explained how kind, comforting and courageous they all were, considering some of the dreadful things they observed. As he was concerned for her and the family, Mum gave him her promise that she would join us in Wolverhampton to stay with Auntie Rose, as soon as the windows and curtains had been replaced, as that was the second time the family had had a lucky escape and she couldn't take chances with the new baby on the way. She thanked her uncle and he replied that he was only "doing his bit for the country" – which was very much in keeping with the attitude of Londoners during the war.

7.   Wolverhampton Once More

When Mum arrived in Wolverhampton with Pat and Albert we all settled down quite well, in spite of the fact that so many of us were squashed into a small semi-detached, three bedroomed house. I believe Jackie shared cousin Miriam's room, but Pat, Albert, Mum and myself all had to share the third bedroom. Of course, life was very different in Wolverhampton. The junior school which Pat and I attended bore absolutely no similarity with the old GLC building we attended in London, which had large coal fires in every classroom, with a huge protective fireguard in front. The teacher's desk was always placed in front of the fire to ensure that pupils were not close to it. In contrast, the Wolverhampton school was a very modern single-storey building, with large windows running along each side, with one side looking out across open green fields and the other onto a corridor running alongside the classes and the school playground on the other side of it. Unfortunately, this lovely building caused a problem because in one lesson we were reading a poem (poetry being one of my favourite subjects; I was completely taken by it)

> *I saw an old woman tossed up in a basket*
> *Twenty times as high as the moon*
> *And in her hand she carried a broom.*
> *"Old woman, old woman old woman," quoth I,*
> *"Wither thou goest up so high?"*

"To sweep the cobwebs from the sky."
"May I come with you?"
"Aye, bye and bye!"

Being an imaginative child with such a love of poetry, I was completely wrapped by it and looked out of the lovely large windows up into the beautiful blue sky covering the fields, wondering where the cobwebs, broom and basket could possibly be. Suddenly my head was jerked back by one of my plaits and a large hand slapped my face with force. The teacher started to rant on about gazing out of the window and not paying attention to the lesson. I was startled and stunned and didn't even try to explain. She wouldn't have listened anyway.

I thought I had better not tell Mum because if we had been in trouble at school, Mum would feel that we had let down the family and would be cross. I needn't have worried, as the children who lived in the same road couldn't wait to tell Mum and she was waiting for me when I arrived home. She asked me what had happened and, rather guiltily, I explained. In reply she said it was all very sad we should forget it had happened. However, unbeknown to me, Mum paid a visit to the Headmistress the following morning and explained that she was greatly surprised that the teacher had not realised that in my London school the windows on the ground floor were covered with sandbags and the upper floor windows were criss-crossed with wide sticky tape. Didn't she understand what London schoolchildren had to put up with? – the noise of the bombing, the sky filled with barrage balloons and aircraft, the warning siren going off any time during the lesson, when they would all fall into line and march downstairs to the ground floor cloakrooms until the 'all clear' siren wailed, causing complete disruption to their lives and education? The Headmistress apologised profusely and Mum left. The following day I was very surprised to see that a completely different teacher was taking our class. There was no sign of the previous teacher and she never appeared again. Mum had quietly done the correct thing without any fuss. It was years later when she told me what she had done.

You see, in Wolverhampton there was very little overt evidence of the war in progress or bombing, apart from the absence of fathers, brothers and sons, who, of course, were involved in one or other of the forces. Rationing was also very noticeable, but I really do not recall any other interference to lifestyle or education, whereas, in our old London school, we were encouraged to be aware of our menfolk fighting for us and, in fact, had frequent knitting lessons (both boys and girls). We knitted sea-boot stockings for merchant seamen. We used four knitting needles, pointed at each end, and very greasy thick white wool to knit in two plain and two pearl rib until we reached the length to the heel. Then the teacher took over and knitted the rest of the stocking from heel to toe. I took great pride in and care with my knitting, as I always thought of the seamen who would be wearing them and the cold, rough and dangerous seas they would be sailing on. Sadly, not all the pupils enjoyed knitting. Each piece was collected at the end of the lesson by monitors and then placed together in a box. When they were handed out by monitors for the next lesson one never knew which piece of knitting one would receive and some stockings horrified me – with great holes and dropped stitches and I would try desperately to tidy them up a bit to make them look neat and wearable.

We very often visited the cinema in Wolverhampton. Auntie Rose was very taken by Betty Grable and her husband Harry James, the famous trumpet player. She had all their records, plus 40s big bands such as Artie Shaw, Paul Whiteman and other popular music of the time. The 40s big bands and their music, plus the appealing films from Hollywood (and some British films) did much to raise our spirits during those difficult, worrying years. I remember seeing the film *Rebecca* in Wolverhampton, starring Joan Fontaine and the young, handsome Lawrence Olivier, with whom I instantly fell in love. I also remember seeing Dennis Morgan in *The Desert Song* with other friends. We were so impressed with the film that we wore our coats buttoned only at the neck, with our arms loosely taken from the sleeves. We imagined that we were wearing cloaks and ran along, galloping as if we were on horseback, singing "ooh arh, ooh arh," re-enacting the film. Ballroom dancing became a very popular and spiritually uplifting experience, both romantically and also very exciting when the Americans brought 'jive' across the water with them.

Many young people of the time lived only for each day, not knowing what to expect the following day. I remember going to the Saturday morning pictures with my friends in Wolverhampton. It was usually absolute mayhem and often the projector would break down, but we thoroughly enjoyed ourselves and eagerly looked forward to the following Saturday performance, as many of the films were serialised.

Life must have been very difficult for Mum, sharing Auntie's house and home with our four child family and Mum expecting a fifth, but I never heard her complain, although sometimes she had to be more strict with us than she wished and I think it was a bit of a trial for Uncle Tom, coming home from work at night with a house full of children. As the time drew nearer to the birth of Robert, Mum slept on a camp bed downstairs in the small sitting/dining room. In fact, she actually gave birth on that camp bed and slept down there from then onwards, with the new baby by her side. It must have been a great strain for her and for Auntie Rose and Uncle Tom. Robert (Bob) was born on 21st September 1944 and we actually stayed in Wolverhampton until well after the following Christmas. Then, as 1945 progressed, Mum realized that the bombing in London was ceasing and more of the war was taking place across the Channel in Europe. She felt it would be safe to go home, so off we went to London in early 1945, thanking Auntie Rose and Uncle Tom for their generosity and kindness.

Bob, who unlike we others, had been a restless baby and cried frequently. Mum felt she must provide him with a dummy, much against her wishes. None of us had needed one previously, but she had to consider Auntie Rose and her family. I remember her first action when we had settled down in the train to London was to take the dummy, throwing it out of the window and said, "Thank God we can get rid of that thing!" As soon as possible when back in London, Mum took Bob to the local family clinic, where it was discovered that the poor baby was getting insufficient nutrition from Mum's milk, of which she had always had plenty of excellent quality and had even been asked to give some to the clinic for other mothers. Apparently, all the stress she had carefully disguised had interfered with her milk production and Bob had to be given an additional baby milk powder.

With his war work at an end, Uncle Tom decided he and the family should return to London. One day Auntie Rose invited me to accompany her on a visit to the East End residents Mum had met at the slaughterhouse. They appeared to be very nice people, living in a Victorian cottage. What confused me was, how did Auntie Rose know them, as clearly she did? Perhaps Mum had introduced her to them. Alternatively had I been confused by the slaughterhouse situation and placed it in Kegworth rather than Wolverhampton? In a child's mind this is quite likely, especially with no sign of Auntie Rose's presence at the time. A rather confusing situation really, but understandable.

8.   Life in London

Life carried on as usual in London and we quickly adjusted to living in our own home again, going back to our old friends and relatives was a great joy. Because Pat was twelve she had to go to a secondary school. She had passed her exams at a high grade and was due to go to a grammar school, but because the war was not yet over, many grammar schools were still out of London, having been evacuated. Pat therefore went to the nearest in-between type of school, which in those days was called a 'Central Secondary".

Being two years younger than Pat, I went back to my previous London junior school, but when I later took the 'Eleven Plus' examination, I too had very good results at grammar school level, I had to go to the same school as Pat as the protocol in education was to place siblings with each other in the same school. There was a slight benefit though, as although I learned Latin and also three years of classics, the school also taught book-keeping, shorthand and typewriting. We were told that the education was to prepare us for a career as a nurse, librarian or secretary. The war certainly interfered with young people's education, but most of us accepted whatever was chosen for us. I'm not sure that would be the case today.

Finally, the war in Europe ended in May 1945. Of course there was still food rationing, which gradually became less, but I know that when I married in 1954 I had to have two ration books (one each), but it was only for a few months and very few articles of food. 'Dig for Victory' was very much in peoples' minds at the time and one of Dad's sisters, Auntie Ruby, who lived in Croydon, had a very large allotment which she had to manage alone as Uncle Stan, her husband, was a serviceman. We even made a small garden patch outside the living room of our council flat, which we children managed, so prevalent was the idea.

I'm not sure if it was the end of the war with Germany, but probably the end of the war with Japan, but what I do recall is my mother and some of her friends and neighbours going round to all of the flats and asking if anyone was willing to give some food, money or food coupons for a "street party". Some people offered food, which they had been hoarding for a special occasion. How on earth they managed it I do not know, but there was one huge, long table in the square, which was absolutely covered with all kinds of food, most of which people had been saving for an emergency.

Our father's piano was wheeled into the square and one of Mum's friends, whose home had been damaged by the same bomb which had damaged ours and had moved to a flat nearby, was willing to play the piano and there was much dancing and singing into the late evening. The joy and release was wonderful.

I was on school journey with my junior school, in Clevedon in Somerset, when the war in Japan was declared over. We were on a walk through a forest, which was a little damp as it was raining and we each had been given an army groundsheet, which could be worn as a rain mac/cloak or floor covering on wet ground, or even used as a tent if two were placed together and strings joined them. It was a strange setting to hear of the complete ending of the Second World War, but it was a great relief. Mum's two younger brothers, Uncle Bob and Uncle John, were serving in the Far East when the two atomic bombs were dropped on Japan. Uncle Bob was with the Royal Army Service Corps in Burma. His job was to drop supplies where required in the middle of the Burmese jungle. He flew in Dakotas, which he found acceptable with English pilots, but he said it was very scary and unnerving when he was with American pilots, because they were 'daredevils' and would fly very low over the jungle and made the plane vulnerable to ground gunfire.

Uncle John was in the navy and when he was in Singapore the army gave leave to Uncle Bob so that he could meet up with his brother. This was quite common but not much known, during the war. Strangely, both brothers died in their sixties with cancer. I've often wondered if there was any connection with radiation from the atomic bombs.

As in Wolverhampton, the cinemas in London were very popular. Of course, prices were very much lower in those days. They ranged from ninepence, one shilling and nine pence, two shillings and three pence and two shillings and sixpence in old money, which equals roughly half of today's equivalent money. There were always long queues of people waiting for the next showing and all kinds of buskers – acrobats, musicians, dancers and singers performing to the queue, As soon as the queue moved forward out would come their hats or plates for people to drop coins into. There was one cinema in the Elephant and Castle, the Trocodero, which, during the showing of a film would suddenly flash a printed message across the screen from someone's son or husband, who was serving abroad and wished to send his love and good wishes to (named) family and friends. This would continue between films, with large photographs of each uniformed serviceman, coupled with their loving messages. The same serviceman and messages would be shown for a week, thus all their families would go to see it. Our family were extremely surprised when Uncle Bob was shown, dressed in his shorts and large hat, suitable for the sun and heat. Word flew around the family and most family and friends made the effort to see him.

If a warning siren was sounded the manager's voice would announce this to the audience and suggest that if anyone wished to leave they may do so immediately. In my experience few people ever left. There were also messages which came up onto the screen stating, "Would so and so please go to the foyer as a member of your family is waiting for you." It could very often be a serviceman on surprise leave!

The war years were a very sad, frightening and emotional time, but I recall very little evidence of avarice or greed and much more community feeling and love and respect, which was probably due to the fact that no-one knew if they or their friends or neighbours would still exist the next day. Of course, there were what were called 'spivs' or 'wide-boys' who dealt in stolen or illegal goods but I suppose every country has similar kinds of people, mainly men, although I did know of a local lady who could get clothes on demand. The spivs and wide-boys were often young men who had managed to dodge being 'called up' to serve in one of the services or were 'on the run', having deserted from the forces and being sought by the military police. Of course, they had to make a living somehow. When things are scarce it is always a temptation to steal and this is encouraged by those who wish to buy such goods. These people operated in what was called at the time the 'black market'.

Our flat was on the ground floor and immediately above us on the second floor was what was known as 'the washroom'. This was one huge room, the size and shape of our complete flat, with no glass in the window frames, just iron bars, which allowed the wind and fresh air to enter. There was a sink with a tap and multiple metal poles with washing lines running from one pole to another. Each flat was designated a certain area. The washroom was very well used, as there was little room in the flat to dry clothing. Mum always placed her week's washing in there to dry. It was usually left all day and overnight.

Imagine everyone's surprise one morning when they went to the washroom to retrieve their laundry, only to discover that the room was completely empty. I know that Mum was heartbroken. She had lost all the linen and towelling of the house, plus our under-clothing and top clothes. Pat and I were very upset as Mum had saved up her money and coupons to buy us a new dress each and we had only worn them once before they went to be washed. Most mothers were in a similar position. No-one had a lot of money and coupons to spare and most of the washing was irreplaceable.

Mum's little grocery shop, which she had attended for many years since her marriage, was frequently burgled, which was very sad, as the owners were such a friendly, helpful couple who always tried to assist Mum (legally) if she required something special. I know that if you saved ration coupons given for one type of food, they could be used for something else. I remember clearly that Mum kept coupons (which I believe were possibly for sugar) to exchange for dried fruit and candied peel etc, as were required to make Christmas puddings, whenever they were available and the shop owners would advise her, which she would save up until Christmas was approaching, as obviously, these goods were very rarely available.

One year, as Christmas was approaching Mum sent Pat and I to the local Off Licence of the pub just around the corner armed with a jug, to buy a jug of ale. Then we all sat around her and watched her mix all the ingredients together. She then asked each of us in turn to stir the ingredients slowly, one by one, suggesting that each of us make a wish as we stirred. We probably all wished for an end to the war, or for our father's return home, but we were not to tell the others what we had wished for, as that would have broken the spell. Such lovely childlike innocence! When Mum had finished making the pudding mixture, she spooned it into several basins and each basin had several clean, shiny silver thre'penny pieces. If any of our family found one in their Christmas slice of pudding, then we had to return it to Mum, who would give us the equivalent in the present day coinage, as silver thre'penny pieces were extremely rare.

A week or so after making the puddings, Mum would place them in the large stone 'copper', in which we heated up our bathwater. She topped it up with water, as required, then lit the small fire beneath. Thus she had made several lovely Christmas presents for our friends and family, which were rare gifts, as it was very difficult to get the ingredients. Puddings were just another thing you had to go without at Christmas, so Mum's wonderful, caring idea was such a surprise for the recipients, who never dreamed they would be able to have a real Christmas pudding with their Christmas dinner.

My maternal grandmother did something similar when she exchanged some old clothing with what was known as the "rag and bone man", who would walk around the streets pushing a wheelbarrow and ringing a bell, calling out, "any old rags, bottles or bones!" or "any old lumber!" In exchange for the clothing, Nan was given a dozen day-old chicks. I can recall seeing them in a large cardboard box in the coal fire grate, near the fire, to keep them warm. Often I would see a huge cast-iron pot on the gas stove, filled with such things as potato peelings and kitchen scraps, all mixed together with something called Karlswood Spice, which was bought from the Corn Merchant, again using coupons designated for something else (which I believe was eggs).

When the chicks grew stronger, Nan had a chicken hutch and a chicken run built for them in the back yard of her lovely, large Victorian house. At Christmas that year, all the family were given a chicken for a Christmas present. We each had a wonderful roast chicken for Christmas dinner, absolutely unheard of during the war. We knew nothing about turkey in those days; for the wealthy there would possibly be duck or goose, but no-one had turkey. It was amazing how adversity brought the ingenuity and enterprise in people at that time, but each willing to share with others.

Auntie Chris (Adelaide) told me of a very interesting incident. When she came back to London with Great Granny Ward's body, she felt that she would like to become a 'Land Girl' in the Women's Land Army. This was a force of young ladies who worked on farms to replace the young male farm workers who had been 'called up' to join the forces. She had to wait until she was eighteen until she could enlist. This involved having a medical. Unfortunately, Auntie Chris had had rheumatic fever when she was young, which had left her with a murmur in her heart, so she was declared unfit to join any of the forces. She was bitterly disappointed but Grandad, her father, arranged for her to have a job in Waterloo Station bar/cafeteria.

As explained earlier, London was absolutely full of servicemen of various types and countries. The main line stations were particularly crowded, so Grandad thought she would feel she was 'doing her bit for the war effort'. Everyone felt they would do anything they could to help the country in her hour of need.

One day two young soldiers came in and asked for a cup of tea. Whilst waiting they asked Auntie Chris if she knew of anywhere they could stay for the night. They had travelled down from the North and were to join their regiment in London early the next morning. Auntie Chris suggested the Union Jack Club, but they advised her that it was full. She then suggested various other places/hostels taking in servicemen for the night, but again they advised her that they had tried all of them and each one was full. She thought for a while and then asked them if they were prepared to wait for her to finish her hours of duty and she would see what she could do to help them.

Her two brothers were abroad with the forces, so their two beds would be empty and available. When she finished her duty she took the two young men home with her and asked her mother (my grandmother) if she could put them up for the night. Grannie thought about it and then agreed. The young soldiers were over the moon, as they had thought they may possibly have to stay in Waterloo Station all night. They quickly took their kit to their room and came downstairs, when Gran and Auntie Chris offered to show them around London for a while. They were delighted and agreed. They all came home, went to bed and the young soldiers were up first thing in the morning and went off to join their regiment after which Auntie Chris and Grandma went off to their jobs.

Several years later, Grandma heard a knock on the door and, standing there with their two wives, were the young soldiers now, of course, both civilians, as the war had ended. They explained that they had never forgotten Gran's and Auntie Chris's kindness when they were stranded and they wanted their wives to meet the two kind ladies. Grandma explained that Auntie Chris was now married with two children and was living in her own home. They asked Gran to thank Auntie Chris for what she had done for them, and their wives also wished to send their gratitude. There must have been countless small incidents like this during the war, although I might feel a little reluctant to allow two male strangers into my home when there was no other male present, these days, when life is so different. This is another example of the 'community spirit' which seems to arise in an emergency.

I can recall another very humorous example revealing Mum's generosity and community spirit. It was a Saturday morning when the Air Raid Warning began to wail. Soon there was the pounding of guns and explosions of bombs. Mum suggested we all remove to the bedroom/shelter when there was a frantic rat-a-tat-tat on the front door. Mum opened it to find Mr Shushems (well, that is what everyone called him) standing there.

"Please may I come in to shelter, Mrs?" he asked.

"Yes, of course," Mum replied. "We are in this room."

Mr Shushems was the local greengrocer, who was probably on his delivery round with his horse and cart. However, he must not have closed the door behind him. Mum was just about to say "make yourself comfortable and take a chair" when she heard someone else in the hall. She called out, "Please come in. We are all in this first room." When there was no reply and no-one entered, she decided to go into the hall to see who it was and she came face to face with Mr Shushems's horse. It could only manage to get half-way up the hall because the cart was preventing full entry! Mum patted his nose, saying, "There, there dear, just stay there for a minute." She then called to Mr Shushems and together they unharnessed the horse and pushed the cart back into the 'square'. They closed the front door behind them, squeezed past the horse and came into the room with us. The horse stayed in the hall until the 'All Clear' siren wailed. The poor horse must have been terrified when Mr Shushems left him outside alone with all the loud banging and thudding.

Horses were used frequently for business deliveries. There were very few cars about because not many people could afford to buy one and petrol was very scarce and rationed – we walked much more in those days and bus transport was cheap and easily available. There was an occasional small car to be seen sometimes in London, fuelled by some sort of gas, contained in a large bag the width of the car and somehow fixed on to the roof.

Horse manure was quite frequently seen in the road and people would shovel it into a container to use as compost in their gardens. I recall the Ballards frequently sending Pat and I out to the street with a bucket and shovel to pick up the horse manure for the garden. There was no way that they would do such a thing themselves, it would have been degrading for them.

9. After-effects of War

There was dancing in the streets and great celebration in London when the war ended, but there are always two sides to every story. It was now time to mop up the terrible devastation that had been caused – so many bombed-out buildings – and there was still food rationing and coupons required for food and clothing and other commodities. America, under President Roosevelt, had loaned the government money under the 'Lease/Lend' arrangement but generally there was much poverty. The rebuilding took many years to complete,

But it wasn't only devastation to buildings. Many families had been broken apart by death or emotional breakdown due to the war. On occasions a husband came back to discover another man living in his home with his wife and family. Others discovered that their wives had borne children whom they had not fathered. Others felt unable to return home because they knew they couldn't handle the life they had before the war. Some even committed suicide because they couldn't live with the terrible things they had observed. Many prisoners of war, particularly those who had been in Japanese prison camps, were suffering from starvation and near to death. Few families returned to anything like the life they had previously led.

As for us, of course we were very happy and excited, looking forward to our father's return home. Certainly, he looked very smart when he arrived home, wearing a new 'utility' suit, a trilby hat and a beige mackintosh. He had also been given £30 to help to cover the loss of earnings. Unfortunately, what the authorities were unable to do was to repair the damage that had been done to his health, both physically and mentally. The charming, happy, loving husband and father who had enlisted in the forces was now so different. At first he soldiered on valiantly and returned to work immediately, only to discover that the promotion he had been promised had been given to a colleague who had not been 'called up', for whatever reason. Dad didn't say much about it, but Pat and I and Mother, of course, knew that he had long planned to buy his own house, as all his family had been raised to do. Now he discovered that because of the war he was returning home to a council flat and with a larger family to provide for. He felt strongly that he had let us all down, whereas we were quite happy living there. The neighbours were mostly quite respectable, friendly and polite and we mixed well with their children.

It was the night-times that revealed Dad's emotional state. He would have dreadful nightmares and would scream out loudly and sometimes sob in his sleep. He would rarely talk about his experiences abroad. Although he had originally joined The East Kent Regiment and was based in Kent, while the 'D' Day landings were being planned, the Army had invited men to join the Royal Army Service Corps to drive vehicles across Europe, which Dad had responded to.

We learned (very much later) that he had been sent up to Scotland to learn to drive a three-ton lorry. For the 'D' Day Landings, a prefabricated floating harbour was invented, called 'Mulberry Harbour'. It was made of floating concrete sections which were towed across the Channel and joined together at the Normandy beaches to form a floating roadway to allow vehicles to drive from the ships to the shore. Unfortunately, the sea was rough and the floating causeway was very unstable and dangerous for the lorries as they drove from the ship. On one occasion Dad let slip that they had been instructed to carry on driving whatever occurred. Unfortunately, Dad's best friend was driving in front of him when his lorry suddenly lurched to the right with the swell and plunged into the sea. Dad watched him sinking but was forced to carry on driving and could do nothing to save him. Dad did not like to discuss his experiences but on very rare occasions something would trigger it and he would reveal something that had been worrying him.

Once he told us that he had helped clear a concentration camp. He may have said Belsen, but I can't be absolutely sure. Again, he revealed a story which clearly disturbed him. Apparently, he was driving his lorry, filled with refugees plus people from the concentration camp, along a road that ran beside a forest. A colleague was also driving a similar lorry behind him. Suddenly they came across a Russian camp and the guards, with guns, stopped them and ordered them from their lorries. They behaved in a friendly manner, calling them 'comrade' and suggested they go to the camp for a drink. Dad said he had refused because he didn't trust them. They then suggested he take a break and go for a walk and have a cigarette, which he did, as he had no option. He soon heard firing, which he had half expected, and he returned immediately, only to discover that the people they had been carrying had been ordered out of the lorries, taken further into the forest and shot. It broke his heart and he lived in guilt all his life, but there was nothing he, or his colleague, could have done. I can still hear his screaming in my mind.

Eventually this all took its toll on his health and he was extremely ill with pulmonary pneumonia and congestion of the lung. Mum was so caring with him, but it really was touch and go. He was finally treated with what we were told were the first penicillin tablets, which were called 'M&B tablets'. Probably the name of the manufacturer, which we knew absolutely nothing about in those days. Sadly, Dad proved allergic to them and his mouth and face were soon covered with sores and scabs. He was in a very bad state. The doctor decided that Dad should go away for convalescence for several weeks, which he did. I believe it was to friends in Scarborough. Today, he would have been hospitalised, but that was very rare in the forties. Nor did the Army concern themselves with aftercare. I strongly believe it was Mother who saved his life. I thank God that the NHS was introduced in 1948 and only hope that it will continue to exist for many years to come.

Dad eventually recovered and carried on a reasonably normal life, but never really the same as before the war or when he built the Anderson shelter for us nor when he collected us at Kegworth and took us on the steam train to London. I'm very sorry for my two brothers, who never knew Dad as he had originally been and didn't even know or recognize him when he returned from the war. Bobby was too young for it to bother him too much – he was probably about 17 months old when Dad returned and was too young to worry, but it was different for Albert, as he was older, about 4 years, and was more inclined to resent Dad coming into and altering our way of life. Father was a stranger to him and it very much showed in their relationship. It was a difficult situation for everyone and I'm sure this could be multiplied thousands of times.

On a brighter note, Dad told us of his once being called to see his officer, whose job it was to censor all the letters coming to and from the soldiers. He did this by blacking out words which implied secret information. He wanted to tell Dad how interesting he had found the letters between him and Mum, which occasioned him to save them until he had finished reading all other letters. He would then sit down, relax and enjoy reading the contents of these letters. I did see some of Dad's letters, which Mum received. They were covered with blacked out words. Mum kept them for years.

Mum never knew where Dad was once he left the East Kent Regiment. It was obviously kept very secret. She had to send her letters to a given army address, where, I assume all the letters were sorted out to go to their various destinations. This meant that Mum and Dad would go weeks without hearing from each other. They would then receive half a dozen letters all at once. Dad knew he wasn't allowed to let Mother know where he was, but rather cleverly wrote in one letter, "There are two eyes, such blue eyes smiling at me". He knew Mum would understand, as the rest of the sentence is "somewhere in France with you". It was a song he had often played on the piano, with them both singing a duet together. Although he had omitted the last part of the sentence, he knew Mum would understand what he meant as soon as she read it, which she did. She said to us, "Your father is in France, but we must keep it a secret between ourselves. Do not let anyone else know." She was so pleased and relieved to know. It must have been a terrible worry not knowing where he was.

Dad was a very talented musician with a lovely tenor voice. He could play any instrument he came across, but it was the piano he loved best. He asked Mum to promise that she would ensure that we had piano lessons whenever we were home in London, which she did. I remember Pat and I having piano lessons quite young, probably between six to eight years old. It was likely to be when he had brought us home from Kegworth.

Our piano teacher at that time was a young married lady who lived in a flat in Blackprince Road on her own. She loved teaching us and always invited us to stay after we both had had our lessons. She would then play a piece of classical work that she was studying. I clearly remember her playing Beethoven and suggesting that we watch her finger movements in particular. On the top of the upright piano, immediately facing the place where one would sit, was a photograph of a young serviceman in uniform. We asked her if it was her husband and she just nodded in agreement. It must have been sad for her to live alone without him and not know where he was. I often wondered if he was still alive, as she wouldn't mention him.

Music played an important part of my life, both classical and the modern music of the time. I remember at our London junior school we listened to a radio programme entitled, "Religious Programmes for Schools". I believe it was on a Tuesday morning. It was the music introducing the programme that caught my attention. It felt so deeply spiritual – far more so than the content of the lesson. Many years later I heard it again and I'm pretty certain it was Barber's Adagio, or something very similar. It is still one of my favourite pieces of music, very moving, but also bringing back sad memories of the war years, but with a deep feeling of spirituality and peace.

Most people are aware of the startling photograph of St Paul's Cathedral standing tall and firm, surrounded by the smoke and flames from nearby bombed and burning buildings in the City and the East End. It was taken quite unexpectedly by a young journalist who just happened to be in the vicinity at the right time. The photograph was immediately taken up by the press to represent a symbol of Britain and its people – stoic, strong and reliable in adversity. Seven years after the war, when I was seventeen, I left college to work in the City of London. I often spent my lunchtime walking around Cheap Street and the area around St Paul's.

Surprisingly, the bomb-damaged buildings still had not been repaired. It was suggested that it was because a very rare species of the Redstart (possibly a Black Redstart, not native to this country), was seen nesting in a bombed building and therefore building and repair work was delayed out of respect for the bird. I often wonder if lack of funds may have added to the delay. Whatever the truth, what really impressed me was that Nature had taken over and all the sites were covered with wild flowers, grass, nettles and all manner of greenery, proving how, if left to her own devices,

Nature soon brings her own order and beauty to what humankind has destroyed.

For most of my life there has never been a time without war, or the threat of war, somewhere in the world. Even now some of our young men are being killed in far-flung Afghanistan and civilians and innocent children are being killed all over the Middle East and Africa, not to mention those killed in the Falklands and Iraq. I recall the song sung by Marlene Dietrich, "When will they ever learn?" Unfortunately, there is a major war facing us at this moment, far more serious than any war that has ever been, the end of which will decide the world's final fate!

A year or two ago a gentleman wrote to a local newspaper to the effect that Mankind had a wonderful mind, having travelled to the moon and back, and has created wonderful inventions. Of course, he did not include the invention of nuclear weapons – had he forgotten? He felt it wasn't necessary to believe in God – religion was the cause of all wars. This statement amazed me, as it showed total lack of awareness of Mankind's true qualities. It is not religion per se (from whatever culture) which creates war. It is humankind who uses religion as an excuse (even fooling ourselves) for why we are destroying Nature and killing each other. It appears to me that ignorance of our own darker qualities – avarice, greed, hatred, jealousy, the desire for power, control and land are the real causes of war.

10.   Afterthoughts & Conclusions

Some time in the late fifties or early sixties, my husband and I saw a film "Nine Hours to Rama", in which a young man shot and killed the peace-loving Mahatma Gandhi, in the name of religion. This caused me great concern and I wondered what sort of God existed, or if It/He/She actually existed at all. I had attended the Christian Church when I was young because in those days one did what one was told to do. I never thought to question religion at all. It was something we were taught to believe, but the young man had killed in faith. How could he believe in a religion which taught one to kill? This, plus my own war experiences and a need to understand, set me on a search for Truth. By chance (or synchronicity) I was directed towards C.G. Jung's Analytical Psychology.

This is not the place to comment too much on Carl Jung's discoveries, but it is necessary to touch on some of them. Freud did a wonderful thing when he discovered the unconscious, but Jung went much further. He discovered that the ego – consciousness – grew out of our unconscious. For example, babies are born completely unconscious, only calling themselves 'he' or 'she' (never 'I') until approximately the age of two or possibly three, being completely unaware of their own separation from other objects or of the ego – 'I'.

Freud's unconscious contained things that we had rejected or forgotten. Jung called this the *Personal Unconscious*, which had developed from a much deeper unconscious, which he called the *Collective Unconscious*.

Consciousness, the Ego, had taken a million years to evolve from the collective and we all carry an enormous 'tail' of collective unconscious around with us, completely unaware of its presence. Occasionally (or even frequently) it influences us without our being aware, both individually and collectively. Our psyches have a light and dark side (a Yin and a Yang). Often we project our dark side onto others, being completely unaware of our own evil but recognising it in others. Jung called this *'Projection'*. One could possibly equate this with Jesus's reference to the 'mite' in the other's eye being seen, but not the 'mote' in our own, but with some differences. For my part, I see the symbolism of the eviction from the Garden of Eden (Paradise) as a wonderful way of describing the growth of the ego – consciousness.

Jung used the term 'Self' for that part of the psyche that unites the conscious with the unconscious, explaining that it contains that which is truly ourselves. He sometimes wrote of it as the 'Christus' or core, which indicates the Christ within us. This is not as strange as one would first imagine. The New Testament in John, chapter 14, verse 16, states:

> *"And I will ask the Father and He will give you an Advocate … the Spirit of Truth … you know him, for he dwells with you and is in you."*

And again in verse 20: "I am in my Father and you are in me and I in you," which clearly refers to the Spirit of Truth dwelling with us and in us.

I have learned now that the Spirit is in everything of Nature, including ourselves and is the source from which our unconscious has grown, which influences us more than we understand, if allowed. It is imperative at this crucial time for the Planet, for us to be still at times, from the noise, hustle and demands of the ego and listen in silence to what the unconscious tells us. Eckhart Tolle, author of "A New Earth" explains this beautifully in the following passage:

"Once there is a certain degree of Presence, of still and alert attention in human beings' perceptions, they can sense the divine life essence, the one indwelling consciousness or spirit in every creature every life-form, recognize it as one with their own essence and so love it as themselves."

Also:

"When you are alert and contemplate a flower, crystal or bird without naming it mentally, it becomes a window for you into the formless. There is an inner opening, however slight, into the realm of the spirit."

The charming young poet John Keats wrote: "Beauty is Truth". Recalling my innocent beautiful experiences during the war, e.g. playing in the wild flower meadow, the feeling of being one with the Universe when looking up through the tiny attic window, the mystical walk from the Oval to our new home as the clock struck midnight and many others since – the sun on the horizon, throwing a golden path towards the coast and myself, hundreds of starlings flying in unison in the sky, soaring, swirling and sweeping in circles, apparently in sheer joy of being, I know to what Keats was referring, and also Eckhart Tolle.

Vine Deloria (2000), taken from Jerome S. Bernstein's "Living in the Borderland", explains clearly how we have abused and ignored Nature and her needs:

> "If you see the world around you as a collection of objects for you to manipulate and exploit, you will inevitably destroy the world whilst trying to control it. Not only that, but by perceiving the world as lifeless, you rob yourself of the richness, beauty and wisdom to be found in participating in its larger design.
>
> In order to maintain the fiction the world is dead – and that those who believe it to be alive have succumbed to primitive superstition – science must reject any interpretation of the natural world that implies sentience or the ability to communicate on the part of nonhumans."
>
> If you objectify other living things, then you are committing yourself to a totally materialistic universe – which is not even consistent with the findings of modern physics."

We know so little about ourselves and a living Nature and seem not to want to know, preferring to do what we think is controlling the Universe, being led purely by ego instincts. Apparently telescopes have been invented that can reach out to planets far beyond our solar system and also technology which can listen to sound from other planets. I'm not decrying such achievements, but it is essential we consider our planet earth before all else, as a priority.

At the moment we are in the middle of the greatest war that has ever existed – the war against our own destruction of the Earth. Both the North and South arctic poles are melting extremely rapidly. Daily we learn of the extinction or near extinction of many plants, fish, insects, birds, bees, butter-flies and much else of Nature. Unfortunately, we appear to be unwilling to change our way of life, making very few, feeble, attempts to show our concern. Few people accept the idea that Earth/Nature is a living being that we are selfishly and unknowingly destroying/killing.

Prince Charles has quite seriously drawn attention to this destruction of the Planet with the deforestation of the rainforests, having visited some of them to observe such major destruction for himself. He has intimated that we will have destroyed Earth by 2017 and has created 'The Prince's Rainforest Project'. I quote from his booklet:

"If we lose the battle against tropical deforestation, we lose the battle against climate change. Please join me in trying to save the rainforests – for the sake of our children and our grandchildren."

Before he died Carl Gustav Jung stated, "Man has nothing to fear but himself." How very, very true.

Many readers may disagree with what I have discovered in my search. That is their prerogative. I apologise if anyone is offended, but we each have to learn what is right for our-selves in life. As far as I am concerned, my search for Truth led me to discover that the Spirit of Truth represents the Holy Spirit, GOD, which is the Source, the Life Force, the Energy in everything of Nature, including ourselves and our Planet. There is a Latin phrase – *Vocatus atque non vocatus*

Deus aderit (Invited or not invited, God is present). That is what I have discovered and now live by.

Today we seem to be moving further and further away from understanding ourselves and our motives. With the growth of technology (not a bad thing, if used wisely) it seems that we do not even have to think for ourselves, we just press a button with one finger, touch a piece of glass and wait for the iPad , laptop, computer, mobile or whatever to give us the answer. I once read the book *Supernature* by Lyall Watson in which he describes a true story of two computers which had accidentally been left switched on during the night whilst the office was closed. The next morning it was discovered that the two computers had been communicating with each other. He suggested that perhaps technology would one day take over our minds, considering all the knowledge that is floating about in the atmosphere from phones, computers, laptops, iPads, etc – so much more information than one mind could contain, which is a very scary thought.

In February 2012 the BBC changed their television reception to digital. Although we had a digital television we still had to ring an 0845 number for advice. We were told to press Menu and then Auto. Suddenly the screen was covered with smears, voices and faces, etc. When I described this to the young adviser he suggested that I need not worry – "the machine is just trying to find the correct reception for you." When then I explained to him that I felt that the machine was using its own mind and I had to just wait and watch, he agreed with me. He also agreed when I said it was rather frightening and intimidating, bearing in mind the fact that in 1997 a computer beat top Russian chess player Garry Kasparov in their second match, after losing the first. Mind controlling?

Most young people's technological games seem to involve destroying or killing to enable one to be the winner. After the young people's riots – burning, stealing and destruction all over England during the summer of 2011 (largely encouraged by contact with each other via mobile phone or computer), when questioned as to why they did such things, many of the culprits claimed that they enjoyed doing it – it was for fun – and they would like to do the same again. It is very worrying that most of our young seem to have lost all sense of reality.

In England, in one month (January 2012) over 900 young children were placed into care, largely due to abuse and neglect. We are destroying our young, who appear to have no moral understanding or guidance. It seems that information technology has lifted our heads into the clouds and our feet are no longer on the ground.

Is this what our parents and grandparents fought and sacrificed themselves for during the Second World War? I think not!

It seems we are racing like lemmings towards our own self-destruction and that of the Planet, but it doesn't have to be like this. Our superficial values seem to be based on materialism – trying to make a lot of money, if not by work then by any other means available. Money is a priority today along with status, position, notice and respect by media and the general population. Is this really of much value when the lives of ourselves and our Planet are at stake? I refer, once again, to Vine Deloria and her reference to our treatment of the Earth and her natural beings:

"If you objectify other living things, then you are committing yourself to a totally materialistic universe, which is not even consistent with the findings of modern physics."

This is what we appear to have become.

Our respect for and treatment of animals is very low grade and selfish. We have refused to accept that animals have their own style of thought systems and communication and accept that they are here only for our use. In fact, we treat most of Nature in the same way. One only has to observe how elephants behave when one of their kind dies. They stay by their side for some time and mourn them. Or, if, when walking along a trail they come across the remaining bones of a dead elephant, they nurse them, stroke them and presumably mourn for them. We are not sure why they do this, but it is very obvious that it is extremely meaningful for them and is an expression of emotion – Love? The Holy Spirit? Should we really house thousands of chickens in one large barn and call it 'free range'? One only has to observe a ewe's treatment of a newly born lamb. The first thing she does is to lick its face to clear its nose and mouth to enable it to breathe. Is this just instinct or a form of knowledge and Love?

Perhaps we need to encourage our young to understand the reality of Nature by drawing attention to natural things more frequently when they are very young and receptive – a walk by a river, canal or lake, if available. A walk in a local park, perhaps with a wildlife book, which can be borrowed from a library, looking for species of birds, plants, insects, fish, etc, which could encourage them to learn and take interest in Nature, away from all the technology.

A walk in a woodland or forest is a deeply spiritual experience. I am aware that many schools are teaching children much more concerning Nature, which is wonderful, before it is too late. However, it is a priority that parents are involved as much as possible. Recognizing that there is a spirit in Nature and that Earth is a living, breathing being is imperative. We have very little time left, if Prince Charles is correct, five and a half years, before we and our planet are destroyed. Is the Collective Unconscious aware of this and warning us through our young – a very mind stretching thought?

Jung would never discuss the subject of a God in his writing. He explained that he was a scientist and physician and would not mention the metaphysical, which was not his work. However, when interviewed in the wonderful BBC series "Face to Face", John Freeman asked him if he believed in God. Jung sat quietly thinking for a while and then said slowly: "Believe... er... believe? I don't believe... I *know*."

George Bernard Shaw wrote in *Plays Pleasant and Unpleasant*: "There is only one religion, though there are a hundred versions of it."

There have been many versions of the Spirit in Nature over thousands of years – Osiris, Dionysus, Pan, Orpheus, Bacchus, Mother Earth, Gaia and the Green Man, etc. There are hundreds of carvings of the Green Man's face, surrounded with foliage, in old churches all over the country. Certainly, in the Middle Ages people recognized him and the need to respect the Earth as they realised their food and water was dependant on him. I am fully aware that daily there is much selfless courage, bravery, self-sacrifice, caring and kindness taking place, which is largely overlooked or ignored, or of which we seem to be completely unaware.

If only we all could slow down for a while and give more care, understanding and LOVE to Nature and the Spirit of Nature – i.e. in everyone and everything around us. Thence we may just have time to save ourselves and our planet from destruction. From my own past experience I have discovered that danger and adversity bring out the deepest feelings of care, LOVE and a community spirit which is much required at this moment as we are in the greatest danger period humankind and Earth/Nature can ever face.

In my final chapter I refer to my mother once again. Shortly before she died in 2005, she gave several of us in the family a gift of a framed poem entitled 'Leisure' by W.H. Davies. It is now so relevant, I quote it below:

> *What is this life if, full of care,*
> *We have no time to stand and stare?—*
>
> *No time to stand beneath the boughs,*
> *And stare as long as sheep and cows:*
>
> *No time to see, when woods we pass,*
> *Where squirrels hide their nuts in grass:*
>
> *No time to see, in broad daylight,*
> *Streams full of stars, like skies at night:*
>
> *No time to turn at Beauty's glance,*
> *And watch her feet, how they can dance:*

No time to wait till her mouth can
Enrich that smile her eyes began?

A poor life this if, full of care,
We have no time to stand and stare.

I give below two further quotes:

Love alone can unite living beings
So as to complete and fulfill them,
For it alone joins them
By what is deepest in themselves.
All we need is to imagine
Our ability to love developing
Until it embraces
The totality of man
And of the Earth.
Teihard De Chardin

"The essence of divinity is found in every single thing –
nothing but it exists. Since it causes everything to be, noth-
ing can live by anything else. It enlivens them; its existence
exists in each existent … Nothing is devoid of its divinity.
Everything is within it; it is within everything and outside of
everything. There is nothing but it."
Moses Cordovero (16th Century Kabbalist)

In our Christian religion we could equate the 'essence' with
the Three-in-One – i.e. God, the Father, the Son and the
Holy Spirit (the Spirit of Truth). In Taoism it could be equat-
ed with Tao. Carl Jung very often compared his
'synchronicity' i.e. meaningful coincidence (mentioned on

page 9 with regard to the Memorial in Kennington Park) with the Tao. I am, therefore, ending The Final Warning with a true story taken from 'The Earth has a Soul' (edited by Meredith Sabini), It was told to C.G. Jung by Richard Wilhelm (1873-1930) who is well-known for his translation of the 'I Ching'.

"There was a great drought where Wilhelm lived; for months there had not been a drop of rain and the situation became catastrophic. The Catholics made processions, the Protestants made prayers, and the Chinese burned joss sticks and shot off guns to frighten away the demons of the drought, but with no result.

Finally the Chinese said: *We will fetch the rainmaker*. And from another province a dried up old man appeared. The only thing he asked for was a quiet little house somewhere, and there he locked himself in for three days. On the fourth day clouds gathered and there was a great snowstorm at the time of the year when no snow was expected, an unusual amount, and the town was so full of rumours about the wonderful rainmaker that Wilhelm went to ask the man how he did it.

In true European fashion he said:

"They call you the rain maker, will you tell me how you made the snow?"

And the little Chinaman said, "I did not make the snow, I am not responsible."

"But what have you done these three days?"

"Oh, I can explain that. I come from another country where things are in order. Here they are out of order, they are not as they should be by ordnance of heaven. Therefore, the whole country is not in Tao, and I am also not in the natural order of things because I am in a disordered country. So I had to wait three days until I was back in Tao, then naturally the rain came."

As our society seems, too, to be in a disordered state perhaps we need to get back 'into the natural order of things' and save ourselves and all our brothers and sisters on Earth, which includes all creatures great and small, and especially our Planet, our beautiful Earth.

Further reading on Tao

Light and easy to read

The Tao of Pooh. Benjamin Hoff (1982).
The Te of Piglet. Benjamin Hoff (1992).

For more serious reading

Tao Te Ching. Lao Tzu (1985). Translation and commentary by Richard Wilhelm. Translation into English by H.G. Ostwald.
The Tao of Jung (1996), David Rosen, M.D.

Addendum

It is not surprising to me that the image of the Green Man is making a revival at a time when the Planet is at risk of total destruction. This symbol has been recognized in one form or another for thousands of years throughout the world and it is an image which is once more being brought up from the collective unconscious to draw our attention to the needs of Nature and the prevention of the destruction of the Earth. In England the Green Man has been known by many names – Jack o' the Green, Robin Hood, Merlin and perhaps Shakespeare's Puck and the Irish Leprechaun.

The medieval alchemists (forerunners of the present chemists) spent much of their lives in semi isolation, experimenting and searching to find the spirit in matter. They called it The Philosopher's Stone, which would turn base metals into gold. C.G. Jung studied alchemy for thirteen years and discovered that it was a projection – i.e. finding the Self (wholeness) from the collective unconscious within oneself.

George Herbert (1593-1632) wrote a lovely poem/hymn describing the spirit in everything of Nature, including ourselves:

> *Teach me my God and King*
> *In all things thee to see,*
> *And what I do in everything*
> *To do it as for thee,*

A man may look on glass
And on it stay his eye
But if he pleaseth through to pass
He will the Heavens espy.

All may partake of this
Nothing can be so mean,
That with this tincture, "for thy sake,"
May not grow bright and clean.

A servant with this clause
Makes drudgery divine:
Who sweeps a room, as if for thee,
Makes this and the action fine.

For this is the famous stone
That turneth all to gold
For that which God doth touch and own
Cannot for less be told.

For further reading, I recommend:

- *Green Man – The Archetype of our Oneness with the Earth,* William Anderson and Clive Hicks (1990).
- *The Green Man – Spirit of Nature.* John Matthews (2002).
- *The Earth Has A Soul – The Nature Writings of C.G. Jung.* Edited by Meredith Sabini (2002).
- *Living In The Borderland – The Evolution of Consciousness and the Challenge of Healing Trauma* (2005).
- *From The Bottom of The Pond.* Simon Small (2007).
- *A New Earth – Create A Better Life,* Eckhart Tolle (2006).